red
Wat

Chris J. Thomas

CAPALL BANN PUBLISHING

www.capallbann.co.uk

Sacred Welsh Waters

©Copyright Chris J Thomas 2004

ISBN 186163 151 0

ALL RIGHTS RESERVED

No part of this publication may be reproduced, stored in a retrieval system or transmitted in any form or by any means, electronic, mechanical, photocopying, scanning, recording or otherwise without the prior written permission of the author and the publisher.

Cover design by Paul Mason
Internal pictures by the author

Published by:

Capall Bann Publishing
Auton Farm
Milverton
Somerset
TA4 1NE

Dedicated to the memory of

Wuggles

Who really cared.

Acknowledgments

Without the assistance of a large number of very kind and helpful folk this book would contain many more misinterpretations and unwitting mistakes than it does. Not being a Welsh-speaker (I've tried - believe me, I've tried!), special thanks are extended to Myra and Cliff James, Mr John Evans and Mr Gwylim Moses who lent their expertise in counteracting the potential damage being done by my wide-eyed innocence of the oldest language in Europe.

Much appreciation is also sent to Mr Jarret Hughes and Mr Davies of Pontllyfni, Mr Peter Nash of Margam, Mr Giraldus Jenkins of Cwmtwrch, Miss Sankey-Barker of Llangattock, Mr Cyril Owen of Cerrigydrudion, Mr Price of Skenfrith and the (literally) hundreds of other helpful people whose local knowledge of history and legend has been unstintingly shared.

Abject apologies are also due to those patient friends and colleagues who spent hours on end enduring my droning on and on and on and on about springs and wells.
My thanks to you all.

Diolch yn fawr.

About the Book

"Sacred" springs and wells may be subdivided into several types - the so-called "holy" wells, those concerned with "healing", wells once considered to have other (usually supernatural) powers and various other sorts. They have all been sacred to some group in some way or another in the past. The main body of the book is a list of springs and wells in alphabetical order of the names by which they are most often identified. There are a handful which, although being used simply for domestic purposes in their heyday, have been included due to their interesting construction. These are not known to be "sacred" in any sense of the word.

None will be placed in any order of subjective importance. "Holy" wells occupying a prominence in the minds of some will not necessarily have the same significance to those who are more interested in "healing" wells, for instance. No banner is carried either for the atheist or the religious fanatic. Despite this stricture, it cannot be denied that most Welsh wells are known today by the names of the saints to which they are dedicated and the list will reflect this. Any perceived irreverence or flippancy will only exist in the mind of the reader. More than adequate compensation for this point of view will be found in other parts of the text, hence ensuring overall neutrality.

Intensive research has involved digging through heaps of obscure literary references, hardly one of which can be trusted to possess a decent provenance. So little has been recorded from earlier ages that no information can be fully relied upon. It would seem that the old tales and beliefs have been passed down by word of mouth until some historical writer or other picked a few up and recorded them in relatively recent times -

historically speaking, that is.

During the course of investigating for this book, the author's feeling towards springs and wells has gradually evolved from an interest, through fascination to a near-obsession. All but a very few of the sites described in the main body of the book have been personally visited. It has been a painstaking and occasionally strenuous process at times, but extremely rewarding and worthwhile. There are many sites far off the usual tourist tracks and, by following the directions, "wellers" will find themselves visiting parts of Wales they would never otherwise have seen except by accident or getting completely lost.

Altogether a total of over four hundred sites where a notable spring or well is alleged to exist have been visited or searched for. Of these, less then half can be confirmed as being still there in some form or other. This is not too surprising when one thinks about it: land drainage, religious intolerance, vandalism, water table depletion and sheer indifference have all taken their toll. Indeed, it is surprising that so many are still left, though many of these are in a piteous condition at the time of writing.

Those which were not located with any reasonable degree of certainty (and therefore not included in the following list) could actually be simply hidden: many could still be there - somewhere. Researched directions to locate them were often so vague or ambiguous as to be totally useless and even when standing right alongside some sites it can be impossible to see them, such is the state of their neglect or total covering by dense thickets. Being unable to find a once-important spring about which much is known (except for exactly where it is) can be frustrating at best, besides taking up a lot of time before reluctantly writing off the site as "lost".

Another aggravation has been the number of sites which are on private land without any public access, but when a spring or well is in somebody's back yard it is not right to go trampling all over their property unless there is a public footpath passing very close by. Still, it's a shame. It can, after all, be justly argued that such sites are the rightful heritage of all of us, not just the landowner's. Worse, paranoid warning signs like "Keep out - or else", "Never mind the bull, beware the owner" or "Intruders will be slaughtered and eviscerated on sight" are enough to inhibit the most innocent of ramblers from venturing any further.

This is why so many important wells have had to be left out and only those in this category which are actually marked on the OS maps have been included with a brief description and any stories. Those listed in this book are generally within easy reach.

Many hundreds of interesting conversations and interviews have been held with inhabitants of the villages which were visited in pursuit of authentic local stories, legends and beliefs. It can therefore be safely assumed that those recorded in the following pages are the result of personal questioning and therefore pretty well up to date as much as possible.

The reason there are a few not personally visited is that nowadays the author has neither the stamina nor the physical fitness he had in his distant youth, so they were effectively beyond his reach. Local enquiries, however, went a long way towards rectifying this deficiency and it is hoped the relevant descriptions of these few are reasonably accurate as far as they go. The number involved is less than a handful, anyway.

A close inspection of the 1:50,000 Ordnance Survey maps will show many other springs, usually marked in blue, which are prefixed with the word Ffynnon. It will also be noticed that they are invariably situated at the sources of streams in the high mountains far away from any possibility of vehicular access other than by helicopter. These have not been included for the same reason, besides the fact that rarely do they have any known historical or religious significance. They are simply springs with a name which mark the source of a stream, that's all, though at one time some may have had great importance to our ancestors. Unhappily, in spite of the fact that many have standing stones and other pagan artifacts very close by, we shall never know for sure.

During his extensive travels researching for this book, the author has been constantly surprised at the interest engendered among people about their own local spring or well once the subject was brought to their attention. Yet so many of the sites visited have been neglected, damaged and even deliberately vandalised it is pitiful to view them. One cannot help but wonder how much is down to apathy and how much is a "Why should I tidy it up for others to despoil?" attitude.

On-the-spot questioning has created some sympathy for this latter view yet there are other springs and wells which have been done up like the proverbial million dollars. Some (like Stinking Well in Cwmtwrch and Gumfreston churchyard) are brilliant examples of what can be done with a little tasteful care and some small funding. Several administrative bodies look after other sites - Local Authorities, the Welsh Office, CADW and other bodies dedicated to the preservation of our history and heritage. Some others are kept in good repair by the good works and devotion of local individuals.

The Millennium has now passed but the occasion has encouraged several communities to restore their local sacred water site. As a result, several of the entries may be virtually unrecognisable from the description given since they were visited by the writer before restoration commenced. This can only be to the good and it is to be hoped many other communities or individuals will do the same rather than wait until the next Millennium.

The author, during his research travels, has persistently tried to instill the idea that bringing the local well or spring up to date for visitors to enjoy (and also to recognise the religious or historical qualifications of these sites) would be worthwhile. This suggestion has been welcomed wherever it has been mooted but obviously the project is too much for any single individual to organise.

A plea, then, directed at all those who read this book and tend to agree with the spirit of the sentiments expressed herein. Why not do your own bit for local history and culture no matter what religion you embrace. Don't forget, your personal ancestors were the same knuckle-dragging thugs as those of the rest of us. Get a few other like-minded individuals together and organise a working party; put up a signpost from the nearest road for the benefit of visiting "wellers"; ask for enthusiastic volunteers from the local school children and make a school project out of it; sort out easy access and tidy up the approach paths. There needn't necessarily be much actual physical work involved or cash needed but where there is start up a local fund or search around for cash from anywhere you can think of.

Small-scale projects seem to be out of favour these days; professional and commercial sponsors only seeming to want to throw bags stuffed tightly with tax-allowable cash at big, prestigious schemes which stand out as grandiose monuments to their cynical marketing philanthropies. But look at all the springs and wells in this book, remember that there are very many more which the author has not managed to locate, but which you may know of, and then think of the huge number of sites throughout Wales or any other part of the country which would benefit. No, it's not a small-scale project at all: it is a huge undertaking made up of lots of little bits, each one of which will go some way to improving the local pride of the smallest of communities.

Take the opportunity to do your bit now - you'll have to wait nearly another thousand years for the next chance of any appropriate significance.

All sites have been given an adequately precise map reference to help you locate them. The map of well sites included in this book will give a reasonably explicit idea of which part of Wales to look for any particular well. However, it is recognised that not every reader will have all the necessary maps for the whole of Wales, so each entry also includes directions of roads, lanes, footpaths and approximate distances which will hopefully enable enthusiastic well-seekers who only possess a large-scale road map to find them relatively easily.

Now look through the list, make your choice of where to go first and GOOD WELLING.

Introduction

Wales, like the other Celtic enclaves of Ireland and Scotland, is cluttered with ancient monuments; they seem to be everywhere one goes. Great castles tower on crags and close to important river crossings. Strange unnatural mounds mark the sites of wooden stockades and earthwork where conflict and death were common visitors. Stone circles stand in places our ancestors revered and where they worshipped their gods. Lonely monolith brood, timeless in their solitary indifference to the petty affairs of Man. Tumuli, cromlechs, hill forts and other traces of primitive natives litter the Welsh soil.

Some are big, most are impressive in some way or other. Preservation being the fashionable order of the day, many are now being made accessible to the public. Yet there is one type of ancient monument which is almost ignored - except by those who possess a true sense of affinity with the history of their country.

Perhaps this is because they are invariably small in size and not considered so worthy of preservation compared with the larger and more popular mouldering heaps of ruins. Being small means they are frequently overlooked and tacitly deemed inferior in some way. The Rev E. J. Newell put it beautifully in his excellent history of the Welsh church - "Familiarity often breeds a measure of contempt and they are not always treated with that reveration which such precious and ancient monuments of antiquity deserve."

Yet the grander and more obvious "monuments" are infants in the time-scale of human history. Those under discussion in this book pre-date them by thousands of years - in many cases probably right back to the time our wary forefathers crept shivering and hungry from warmer climes, following the retreating ice northward.

These are old enough but they are still juvenilles compared to some of the incredible ancient sites found in south Wales and the West Country. The great British Ice Cap never covered this area. Tundra conditions existed in the Gower peninsular and in the Vale of Glamorgan and these sites were probably being used by early Man far back into the last Ice Age.

They are the really ancient monuments, known to some as "well-shrines " or "sacred springs.

They provided the most basic means of subsistence. The earliest settlements were almost totally dependant upon them and in many cases remained so up until very recently. Indeed, a lot of Welsh villages and towns would not even have existed where they now are without them. Upon their locations depends the population distribution of Wales as we know it. Even today a very large number of farms, isolated houses and sometimes whole communities still depend upon them - but their intrinsic importance is far greater than that.

The species of Man, in common with all other living things on this planet, is constructed mainly of water. There are other bits and pieces mixed in, of course, to hold the lot together - carbon, various trace elements and a bit of mystery - but water constitutes the bulk.

Hardly surprising, really, when you consider that life is said to have originated in the mineral stew of the sea, though this is only one theory among many. If true, it would go a long way to explaining one particular aspect of Man's complex nature.

Man has always been martyr to a fascination with water far over and above his need for it to survive; thronging the hot summer beaches, messing about in boats, sliding down the waves on bits of plank, catching fish for sport. Wherever there is a convenient bit of water will also be found representatives of the species enthusiastically pleasuring themselves with whatever aquatic activity grabs them; be it lazing in the sun or tearing around on jet-skis.

That takes care of the recreational use to which we put water, but deep-down (metaphorically speaking), water means a lot more to us than that. What of the spiritual aspect?

Paradoxically, it is not the vast expanses of the ocean or the foam-filled river gorges and mighty waterfalls we reserve for our visceral communion with water. We may stand in awe of the roaring power of the sea and delight in the grandeur of spectacular aquatic scenery, yet these visible proofs of the strength of natural processes are not particularly conducive to spiritual introspection - as much due to the noise created by large volumes of water in violent motion as anything else.

Water has always been associated with the concept of purity - so is the divine state of any acceptable religion. It is only natural, therefore, that Man's eternal interest with things supernatural and psychic will lead him to indulge such instinctive yearnings in quiet places where his equal interest in water is also present. He will go to where the water is at its purest; to where water emerges from the ground; to sites which were given enormous significance by unnumbered generations of our ancestors; to those little places where the most rudimentary and primeval religions on Earth have their roots. He will be drawn to the virgin source of water in its truest sense.

There are wells and there are springs. Both are primary sources of fresh and hopefully uncontaminated water. But there is a fundamental difference between the two.

Wells are man-made artifacts; narrow pits or shafts dug into the ground in an attempt to gain access to some subterranean commodity such as water, oil or gas, but only the first of these concerns us here.

The general public conception of a water well is a very deep and circular hole in the ground surrounded by a low masonry wall and topped with a windlass; very rustic - and all that. Often there is also a double-pitched roof, usually too small to protect the drawer of water from rain but big enough to divert any bird-droppings which would otherwise fall in and pollute the water. It is difficult to imagine any other use for such a roof other than to impart a romantic aura to such a mundane artifact.

Such is the stereotype seen in suburban gardens and in countless nursery rhyme book drawings of Jack and Jill - the well invariably situated at the very top of the hill in the latter case, strangely enough. It is more likely that the models for the Jack and Jill rhyme used a well further up the hill from where they lived, as some dwellings in outlying mountain areas still do. Any idiot knows it's a lot easier to carry a full bucket down the hill and an empty one up, rather than the other way round.

Practical wells of this stereotype are mostly found in flat, arid areas of the world where rivers and streams are far apart and the only available fresh water must be drawn up in a bucket from a hole dug into the ground. Underlying rock strata tends to act as a natural filter, thus ensuring the purity of the water, and this is why they are even found in older properties built on the banks of rivers - surface water has a nasty habit of becoming slimy and foul during the summer months; even drying up altogether at times. Winter floods are brown with suspended sediment and often dangerous to approach if covered with ice.

Deep artesian wells are generally constant, their very depth and darkness inhibiting the growth of algae and only drying up when the water table becomes too depleted to rise above the bottom of the shaft.

Springs, on the other hand, are natural out-flowings where a valley or gully intersects a layer of impervious rock lying under more porous strata. If the rock layers happen to be relatively level, many springs will be noticed along the valley wall forming a definite "spring line".

When rain falls upon the land surface a certain proportion will always sink in rather than run off directly into a stream and gravity will ensure it continues to trickle down until it reaches a layer of harder or more dense rock. No matter how impervious this layer may be, pressure and folding will create a myriad of cracks and cavities through which the water may reach still lower levels. Up to millions of years may pass before any individual drop of water sees the light of day once more in certain areas.

Mostly this underground water will simply seep out under the subsoil along the spring line and will not be evident to the eye but occasionally, due to the configuration of subterranean weaknesses, a larger volume of water will congregate and emerge at one point and this can truly be called a proper spring. From this point downhill erosion will carve a gully which inevitably widens as more water joins from both banks during periods of rain.

In Wales, virtually any "well" can be properly called a natural spring which has been built around for a definite purpose at some time or other. Not all wells are at the point where the water enters the open air, though. Some, like Ffynnon Peris, for example, have been excavated and retained some little distance from the actual spring to avoid boggy ground and there are a couple of cases where a pool in a river is known as a "well" because some noted person or other simply happened to settle down there and left his or her name to mark the spot.

This, then, is the essential difference between wells and springs for the purposes of this book.

Long before history began to be recorded, waters issuing from the ground were undoubtedly looked upon with some respect if only for the reason that many tasted a lot better than the river water - especially during hot summers. Spring water is generally a lot colder than in the streams among the Welsh mountains too, as many an overheated hill walker will testify. Small wonder then that the earliest permanent camps and settlements tended to be established on high, easily defended sites close to a plentiful supply of sweet and unpolluted water throughout the year. In those days river valleys were invariably swampy and choked with vegetation making access extremely difficult.

It probably was not long before these springs began to be endowed with some sort of religious expressiveness aeons before organised religions appeared on the scene. Practical uses too, besides a supply of the wet stuff. It has been suggested that newly- born babies were immediately plunged into the cold waters at such sites both for the purpose of cleansing them after birth and to ensure they were healthy enough to survive and properly serve the tribe. Weaklings or the sickly would very likely perish at the shock of being suddenly immersed like this and their demise would avoid them possibly becoming a drain on the tribe's resources as they grew older. Could this practice, allegedly still carried on in some of the more remote and still primitive parts of the world, be the forerunner of baptism, one wonders? A practical, though cruel ritual gradually evolving into the familiar modern religious ceremony of purification?

Over time the significance and ceremonial use of the more popular springs would have evolved. Prisoners were tortured and butchered on their banks. The messily - detached heads of tribal enemies were bathed in the "sacred waters" as a token of respect for the defeated. Some of the larger springs (e.g. St Winifred's, Ilston,etc.) could have been used for drowning vanquished enemies in the same way as the famed Mayan "drowning wells" (cenotes). Bearing in mind the shortage of meat on the hoof for a couple of millennia after the great Welsh ice cap melted, it is perhaps not too far fetched to speculate that a killing festival could have been followed by the Stone Age equivalent of a knees-up and barbie of roasted enemy. Disputes within the tribe were often settled by bloody conflict beside the spring and sacrifices to local gods were carried out there. Man's ingenuity couldn't help but up the ante. Human nature being what it is, some form of tribal one-upmanship would ensure a certain amount of bragging to outsiders would take place about the powers of the local spring. This would naturally be encouraged (or even instigated) by the resident healer or witch doctor as a sure-fire way of augmenting his or her assumed powers. Being in charge of an allegedly magical spring was bound to have been a position of high status and a lot safer than aspiring to the chieftainship with all the fighting, scars and paranoia that would entail. There is no reason to suppose that social climber did not exist in the Stone Age as well as today. Specimens of this ilk from both ends of the historical spectrum also have much in common in many other respects, as any cynic will confirm with great passion.

Such is a possible explanation for the beginnings of the importance of springs which has persisted in varying degrees of intensity up until the time the first reservoirs were built to supply piped water - and even since in some cases (eg. Lourdes). Most of the wells and springs identified as having a title can safely be assumed to have obtained their initial recognition during pagan times. Evidence of this is often reinforced by their close proximity to other supposedly "sacred" sites such as stone circles, monolith, tumuli and burial mounds. Others are of relatively recent significance in the sense that little or no earlier use is recorded in legend. Usually the outflow was regarded as owning the same value as the water in the spring, whether it be medicinal or spiritual.

Water is so fundamental to life it that could not possibly be left out of the list of four basic elements upon which early worship was based; the others being fire, earth and wind. Springs, streams, rivers and lakes were all revered to the extent that local deities and gods were associated with them. The Welsh word for spring (ffynnon), for instance, can be found incorporated in many Welsh lake names. With the exception of springs, it is just as likely that the availability of fish and edible water plants would have been the primary attractions of most other waters during pagan times. This theory puts springs into a category of their own; their only (but important) virtues being constancy of supply, potability - and possible portals into (and out of) the underworld.

It is only too easy to imagine the evolution of the mystique surrounding springs, given even only partial truth of the theoretical origins propounded above. Each tribe would attempt to outdo their neighbours with wild claims based upon imagined or contrived evidence - the ancestors of advertising agents, some might say. Rituals would spring up as a natural consequence, increasing in complexity and often barbarity as time progressed. Even up until the time of the Industrial Revolution several Welsh healing springs were looked after by a keeper, usually female and often referred to as the "priestess" or "guardian" of the spring. A respected elder of the locality would normally be selected for this job. Duties tended to be light - keeping watch for unauthorised use, covering the water outlet at night and acting as cashier for offerings from visitors. Several examples of this are given later in the book.

It cannot be disputed that some degree of paganism lurks within all of us no matter how impregnable our outward veneer of civilisation appears to be. If you want any examples just observe the faces in the crowd at any football or boxing match when things are hotting up and you will catch a revealing glimpse of the truth of this statement. Paganism often equates with barbaric practices and one only has to look at what is going on in various parts of the world today to realise how superficial this veneer really is. For all our assumed sophistication we, as a race, are not really all that far removed from our earliest hairy, wild-eyed forebears to whom might was right and if you can't join 'em, beat 'em. As a result, springs (or wells) still hold an influence over many of us which can only satisfactorily be explained by assuming some sort of "race memory" is in operation.

Time passed. Invaders came, sometimes leaving their mark with artifacts, more often just stirring the gene pool for relaxation between bouts of the more serious business of pillage, with few other traces of their existence. Primitive dogmas came into being - and went again - many using the springs as part of their rituals to a greater or lesser extent. The Druids, for instance, utilised springs nearly as often as their better-known "sacred groves".
Then the Romans came to Britain in 55BC and began pushing into Wales about 20 years later. They stayed for a while, later bringing with them eager missionaries representing the first properly organised religion to be known in Britain. This religious influx began during the 4th century after the road network had been completed and it is said that St Martin sent many priests into Wales. Initially they went with a retinue of craft and trade specialists together with a few warrior/labourers; a whole gaggle of 12 men besides the priest. The parallel with Jesus and his 12 disciples is obvious.

Farm animals were also taken along and local tribes taught tradesman's crafts. To begin with, whenever a heathen sanctuary (like a well) was found it was damaged or even destroyed. This unsociable practice often met with some stiff opposition and many of these Catholic missionaries and their followers perished at the hands of un-Romanized barbarians. However, more came to take their place in an unstoppable tide.

With an improving knowledge of indigenous pagan practices, the idea of using existing semi-religious sites and rites gained favour - a ploy which had been known to succeed in other countries the Roman legions had conquered. Rome issued an edict to this effect in the form of a list of suggestions on how to maximise conversion statistics using the native's own beliefs against themselves. The way it worked was this:

1) The specially-trained missionary, often working alone, would choose a site where locals gathered and which appeared to hold significance to them. This would obviously have to be somewhere with enough nearby population from whom to scrounge food and with a reliable supply of fresh water for personal consumption close at hand. Sacred springs and stones fulfiled these requirements perfectly, especially as many monolith and stone circles happened to be in close proximity to springs.
2) A hut or more permanent "cell" would be constructed close to the spring and visitors engaged in general conversation which would then be skillfully steered to religious topics citing perceived similarities between Catholicism and local beliefs, most of which would be centred on the spring or nearby stones.

3) Having gained the tacit (or more likely apathetic) tolerance of enough locals, more regular meetings would be arranged. Congregations grew in size and word spread to outlying districts. Gradually and insidiously the missionary would

assert authority over the attributes of the spring, twisting ancient beliefs into those more in keeping with Christianity and thus beneficial to the Church.

4) Using the labour of the converted, a primitive but more permanent chapel, church or monastery would be constructed to complete the procedure. Catholicism would become predominant.

This would be the ideal programme, of course. In practice things would not have been quite so easy. Disputes would arise with the spring's regular custodian or local tribal chieftain - sometimes resolved by the messy and untimely demise of the hopeful potential usurper. This main Age of Saints continued for over 300 years, the churches gradually taking over the role of a local law court where an abbot would sit in judgement on sinners.

In fine weather it was often the custom to hold these trials by the well associated with the church if it was not too distant. It was probably not long before the belief that people should never quarrel by a well came about as a result of this. In other words, any argument or harsh words from the plaintiff or accused would result in a change of colour in the spring water - sometimes several colours at once in a pretty pattern - to the great detriment of all users. This deadly threat would have been enough to keep the proceedings going in an orderly manner, at least.

Capital punishment was never invoked no matter how heinous the crime; there was a better way - kicking the guilty party out of the Church. When a sinner lost the protection of the Communion he would also lose all his tribal rights, be looked upon as fair game and bumped-off out of season by anyone who fancied doing it knowing they would not be punished for the dirty deed.

Over time, the more successful missionaries extended their spheres of influence. "Holy" men, often devout hermits not officially sanctified by the Church, followed the same procedure with equal profit by taking over the "patch" after the inaugural missionary had moved on. Even the most fervent zealot had to make a living, after all, and could not afford to overlook the food, status and comparative security endowed by offering the Cross to a group of the already converted. A lot of these hermits were older, truly devout priests, abbots and bishops who, having been sickened beyond endurance by the corruption, greed and lechery of their fellow ecclesiastic, opted out of formal Church life and went freelance. As one ancient chronicler delicately put it - Welsh Christians were "corrupt in morals and utterly lacking in religious zeal except such as manifested itself in gloomy and selfish asceticism."

This method of spreading the Word has been pursued in places all over the world but nowhere has it left so much of a mark up until the present day as it has in Wales.

For proof of this take a look at one of the Ordnance Survey maps of Wales (1:50,000 recommended). Now try to count the number of places (villages, towns, farms, etc) with the prefix Llan---. Allow a day or two to do a proper job.

What relevance has this to do with springs and wells, you may reasonably ask?

Every language contains a number of words which are essentially untranslatable; only having meaning as an expression of a concept, idea or implication. Llan--- is one of those words.

Different Welsh-translation dictionaries will give you several different meanings to choose from, depending on which one you refer to. The old usage is "enclosure", which described the mound-and-ditch structures or palisades erected to protect the tribe and its livestock from attack; others are "church", "parish", "village", etc. All come close when used in a certain context but no single word will give a true concept when applied to place-names, especially when the prefix is followed by a personal name, as it nearly always is - and usually a saint's name at that.

To avoid going into too much philological detail, a single typical example should point the way to understanding. Take the name of a small rural village on the north-east coast of Anglesey, for instance - Llaneilian.

Eilian was a saint, not Welsh, who brought his family from somewhere in Europe to convert the heathen Welsh to the Cross. Where he landed he successfully founded a church using the procedure recommended by Rome. A "sacred" spring once used by the Druids provided his focal point.

He died in 583AD and the village still bears his name after more than 1,400 years. Roughly, it means "the parish founded by St Eilian". In essence, it was Eilian's "patch", his "turf" or "catchment area". This is what today's "Llan---" implies when prefixing a Welsh place name. Llanbeblig, the old name for a suburb of Caernarfon, is credited with being the first of the 500-odd "Llan---"s with saints' names scattered throughout the country. Peblig, son of St Helen, founded a church there in 390AD and his name stuck. Those named for the earlier saints are on the oldest Christian sites while those dedicated to St Michael (Llanfihangel---) date from early in the 8th century. Youngest in order of age are those dedicated to St Mary (Llanfair---) which started to become popular towards the end of the 10th century.

Staying for a moment on the language theme, have you ever wondered how the words "spring" and "well" originated? "Well" does not only refer to a water source but also means "feeling good". Could the fact that so many wells were used for healing have given rise to this word which implies a state of bodily contentment - or was it the other way round? Think of how many joined words include "well"; "well-being", "well meant", "well-advised", "well-intentioned or "well-blessed" to name but a few. There has to be a connection. The many well puns (mostly inadvertent) the reader may notice in the list of springs and wells can only serve to reinforce this observation.

It's the same with "spring". Nearly all the powers associated with water-springs are supposed to be at their peak during the re-awakening of life after the chill of winter. So did the name for the season of rebirth come from the word "spring", meaning water from the ground, or the converse? Who can say for sure? "Well-spring" indicates a benevolent source; the "Fountain of Youth" could be associated with the Springtime practice of young people holding festivals at well-sides. References to springs and wells (some admittedly oblique) litter the English language to such an extent that their influence on our linguistic culture must be beyond any dispute.

In the Welsh language, a very much older tongue, the word for both "spring" and "well" is *ffynnon*, which has no discernible common root with well (meaning good and translated as iawn) or Spring (the season, translated as Gwanwyn). The inference is clear; other uses of "well" and "spring" have evolved only in the English language which goes back (in a recognisable form) to shortly before the Romans came a'conquering.

It has been claimed that there are close on 500 wells dedicated to saints and their religious practices in Wales, the majority of which are either impossible to locate definitely or only exist in the minds of amateur historians. Whether this estimate is close or not, the saints were undoubtedly great dedicators in their single-minded efforts to drive pagan practices from their heathen flocks.

There is also a story that 20,000 Welsh saints are buried on Bardsey Island (Ynys Enlli) off the Lleyn peninsular, which was founded by St Cadfan in about 516AD (others say it was 615AD). It is unlikely that they are all together in a mass grave so no amount of excavation will ever prove the validity of this assertion. There weren't as many saints as that, either, a total of 479 having been recorded. More likely the larger number is roughly the number of holy men and other religious refugees who sought sanctuary there when the Saxon massacres were at their peak. Reports of the brutal killing of over a thousand innocent monks at Chester in 617AD may have started the ball rolling. Pilgrimage to Bardsey suddenly got popular. However, the rumour that there are so many saints buried there does have a bearing on the large number of Welsh wells.

During this period "well chapels" were constructed beside, or on top of some of the more popular springs. Canopies and masonry surrounds were used and traces of these can sometimes still be seen today. Shelves and seats were incorporated in the walls for the display of effigies, storage of equipment for the required rituals and offerings from pilgrims. All used the springs and wells for their own purposes, many of which were of a religious or ritualistic nature. The springs remained, eternal and uncaring, serving all with their individual needs whether they be spiritual, clinical or therapeutic.

Each spring or well became endowed with its own ritualistic properties, many of which originated in pagan times and, in a few cases, are still observed today. For instance, water drawn from three separate wells in the same jug before sunrise on a Sunday could be used for magic. If it was drawn before sunrise downstream of any spring on Easter day it would guard the pilgrim against evil spirits and witchcraft for a full year and if drawn in the hour before mid-day at Christmas or Easter, not only would it turn into wine but would also be at its most efficacious for the colic and any other stomach pain.

It was habitual on an Easter Monday to dance at certain springs and scatter flowers around the site. This was done to ensure good fortune for the coming year and can only be a hold-over from the ancient Celtic water-worship age just like the taboo against spilling water when carrying it from a well for medicinal purposes - this was seen as an omen of sorrow or loss, boding awful consequences for the sick recipient.

As a matter of etiquette, two or more people wishing to use the same well at the same time would have to draw the sign of the Cross in the surface of the water before doing their own thing, whatever it was. This is evidently not of pagan roots unlike the saying that you should never scatter well water from your hands after washing first thing in the morning or you would scatter all your luck for the day.

Many invasions were made by Danes and other Norsemen in the 9th and 10th centuries. Much damage was done to Christian shrines and churches in this time of brutish conflict but when the Normans turned up they put a stop to all that nonsense and left the wells and springs pretty much alone. Anything to keep the peasants happy. Time rolled on.
Later, in the 16th century, small wood and pottery figurines of saints were carried by nomadic friars to exchange for food instead of money. The favourites were Seiriol and Curig. Seiriol had a powerful reputation of being useful for healing and Curig was tops for keeping evil spirits away from the house.

Then came the Reformation. Priests were killed in many unpleasant ways. Churches and chapels were converted into ruins; well-chapels and many of the wells themselves destroyed. The period was a textbook example of the evils of religious intolerance. But so ingrained was the habit of centuries that the springs and remaining wells were still used, albeit surreptitiously. This period probably gave rise to the custom at some wells of only visiting for healing purposes during the hours of darkness but gradually, as the population began to mass into expanding industrial centres to an ever increasing degree, the number of springs in constant use declined.

A brief resurgence (brief in the active life of a spring) arrived in the 18th century when visiting a spa and "taking the waters" became the trendy thing to do. Money-grabbing entrepreneurs of the age cashed in by building hotels to accommodate enthusiasts of this new fad while local landowners joined in and constructed baths and pump rooms over their springs - and charged admittance, of course.

Mid-Wales, particularly in the Irfon and Ithon valleys, was the centre for this. Owners of springs in other places - some with acknowledged healing properties - tried also. They all failed when compared to the success of the Welsh "Spa Belt", due mostly to poor access by road or rail.

This bonanza faded away in its turn and the remaining evidence of this is to be found in a few parts of Wales. Everything passes, except perhaps the outpouring of the springs. Even organised religion, which had such close associations with underground water sources in the past is slowly losing its hold upon the minds, actions and attitudes of ordinary folk. One probable reason for wells being ignored today is that there is no longer any money to be made from them. Who is going to pay to see a small pool of water no matter how nice the surrounding well-chamber is? Of course, some springs are now being tapped, bottled and sold as "mineral water". These sites are also out of bounds for all practical purposes as an industrial enterprise.

Yet the springs remain, many forgotten, many more destroyed by Man's obsessive interference with a landscape he has no moral right to alter to the extent he does, and others which are still cherished, preserved and improved for the benefit and enjoyment of those who come after.

So many have been filled in, diverted or destroyed in other ways for religious, economic or antisocial reasons. Lowering of the water table by extraction, open-cast mining and land drainage has accounted for the demise of many others but there are still plenty left to admire and use for a spiritual top-up.

To establish and visit the site of an ancient important spring which has been all but forgotten - even to visit one which has been carefully preserved - cannot fail to fill the properly sensitive visitor with an awesome sense of antiquity akin to that found in the vicinity of stone circles and monolith. Even the trees and stones surrounding the spring often seem to be impregnated with an aura of great significance. Some are very special places which once really meant something to our ancestors. God knows they did not have much of a life by modern standards but at least they had their beliefs, which such springs strengthened by providing tangible and visible proof of the validity of their faiths.

People have visited them for countless generations whether it be for healing, cursing, religious or oracular reasons. So many people over so many years, perhaps many millennia. They were places of worship, sacrifice, tryst and assembly. Many grim scenes have been acted out by their bubbling waters - so have many apparent miracles. Fertility rites, exorcism, weather charming, divination; whatever mystical concepts man could dream up, the springs would be involved somewhere along the line. All have their tales to tell; simple, child-like tales for the most part, but those were unsophisticated times. Alas for their passing, some might say.

Most of those tales will never be proven (or otherwise - never forget that). All we have left today is hearsay, local legend, a few facts and a vast array of imaginative fantasy. The springs aren't bothered. They will still be there after the human race has managed to exterminate itself by some means or other, whether it be by slow poisoning, war, pestilence or a mad lemming-like gallop back into the ocean's womb to escape the terrible stresses of over-population. The few survivors will need something to believe in as they lapse back into barbarity after it is all over - and they will also need a constant supply of fresh water.

Who knows? The springs might once more be pressed into a more useful role than that of idle curiosity.

And the whole cycle could start all over again.

List of Springs and Wells

Although the waters of the springs and wells listed below have been drunk by countless visitors throughout the ages for refreshment and healing it must not be assumed that it is completely safe to sample any of them today. Some are crystal clear, as free from any artificial chemicals or contamination as you can get; some are laced with naturally dissolved underground minerals and will do you more good than harm - but others resemble a highly concentrated germ soup when viewed under a microscope. Those which come surging from the ground or run out of a pipe are usually all right but static pools or small trickles must be treated with great suspicion. Like drinking and driving - if in doubt, don't go guzzling the stuff down in bucketfuls.

* Indicates that the well is marked on 1:50,000 OS map.

* St Aeliw's Well? *Anglesey*
(Ffynnon Aelrhiw).
OS Map 123. GR 242 295

A walk of a full kilometre is necessary to see this well - and often more due to the difficulty of parking on the narrow road close to the beginning of the footpath. This distance is why it is one of the very few wells in this book which has not been personally visited by the author - his physique just isn't up to it any more.

The correct names of the saints are often in doubt. So few written records remain from that time, and what there are were usually written so long after the event that nothing can be properly trusted as fact.

There is a certain amount of confusion about this name. One authority suggests there may have been a saint called Aeliw yet the name by which the well is commonly known translates literally as "brow of the hill". Trouble is, the big hill known as The Rhiw overlooks the well. Ho hum, problems, problems. Still, one name is as good as another.

The well is in forestry at the western end of the great sweep of storm beach called Hell's Mouth Bay (Porth Neigwl). A visit here during a strong sou'wester at high tide will explain the name more fully than words could ever do.

From Pwllheli take the A499 along the coast to Llanbedrog and turn right on to the B4413. Follow this to Botwnnog and take the first lane on the left as you enter the village. Take the first left again, go over a rather peculiar old bridge crossing the River Soch and follow this road towards the looming mass of Rhiw Mountain, the remains of an ancient volcano. At the very bottom of the slope, before you start to climb the hill, there is a sharp left-hand bend. The start of the footpath is on the right on the bend.

A private gravelled track leads to "Ty'n-y-Parc" and beyond here is the forestry. Ffynnon Aelrhiw is in the middle of the plantation right alongside the footpath. It is said to be a bit over 3m square with seats around and reputed to relieve various types of eczema.

If you follow the same footpath further there is supposed to be another well by the side - somewhere - dedicated to All Saints. Here, the usual offering by the poor was a simple pin - all they could afford, in many cases. Wells of this sort are to be found all over Wales and many examples are cited later.

* St Alhaiarn's Well ✓

(Ffynnon Alhaiarn).
Festival Day 1st November.
OS Map 123. GR 385 446.

One of the few wells which has easy access for disabled visitors. It is located in a spectacular setting among the range of extinct volcanoes called Yr Eifl (The Rivals) and the waters of this copious spring bubble to the surface near the bottom of a towering slope.

It is about 300m uphill and due west of a church dedicated to St Alhaiarn, a disciple of St Beuno whose "patch" was at Clynnog Fawr only a few kilometres up the coast, and later a hermit.

Travelling south along the A499 from Caernarfon, the B4417 branches off to the right at the entrance to the little village of Llanalhaiarn, which stands in a good defensive position guarding the only practical pass through these mountains. Go along this road to the far end of the village, then a few hundred metres more, and a small masonry building will be seen on the left-hand side of the road outside a house.

The original "sacred well" was located directly opposite on the other side of the road. Such is the purity of the water that it has been confined within a cistern which is used to supply the village. The present well-house was constructed in 1900 due to the fact that the waters were still in demand for uses other than domestic.

A peculiarity of this spring was occasional billows of bubbles from the bottom of the well. This disturbance, unusual in a spring which does not issue from boggy ground, was looked upon as the optimum time for patients to bathe in the well. A masonry seat was erected at the well-side for them to sit while awaiting this most propitious of moments. Unfortunately, as the water now has to negotiate a cistern before being seen, these miracle-working bubbles are no longer in evidence.

The easing of rheumatic pains was one of this well's greatest virtues; difficult to understand when one tests the temperature of the water. A temporary numbing of the discomfort may well have been experienced followed shortly by the need for a further visit when the condition deteriorated as a direct result of immersion in the icy water. Of course, this opinion is based upon modern medical knowledge - different circumstances and outcomes would naturally prevail after the waters had been blessed by a saint.

Ridding a patient of warts was its other claim to fame. Warts must have been rampantly endemic in those days - so many wells were necessary to accommodate all the sufferers in Wales. This particular well required a special ritual to obtain best results, though. A scrap of sheep's wool impaled on a bramble or thorn had to be collected when travelling to the well for treatment. On arrival, the offending wart would be scratched with a pin until it bled, the gory pin polished with the wool then bent and thrown in the well.

This procedure would have to be repeated for each wart the sufferer wished to dispose of. The wool would then be hung on the first sloe bush located on the way home. If all stages had been correctly observed, the designated warts would fade away as the fickle Welsh weather broke up and disposed of the wool.

There was probably a "priestess" collecting fees here, as at most popular wells. Today it is "owned" by the Water Authority and the simple concrete chamber in the building over the road is in private hands, belonging to the adjoining house which used to be part of the church estate. Water is diverted to a container within the garden but most flows parallel to the road back down towards the village.

It is very probable this spring was used for pagan purposes long before Alhaiarn appeared on the scene and founded his church here in the 7th century. The later cruciform village church dedicated to him is built on the same site, a site which pre-dates Alhaiarn's time as a very much older religious place - evidenced by a few ancient inscribed stones within its precincts.

* St Allgo's Well *Anglesey*
(Ffynnon Allgo).
OS Map 114. GR 499 848.

About 3km past Benllech on the A5025, turn left at the roundabout and take the first left again half a kilometre further on. Almost immediately, enter the second caravan site entrance (Glanrafon Uchaf) facing you on the right of the lane, go past the phone box, ignore the decorative stereotype well standing on the bank to your left, and look for a gap in the caravans just a few metres further on the right. Here is the real thing.

A ruin at the time of writing, like so many others, it is hopefully due for resurrection as a valuable extra feature to this well-run caravan site nestling in a small pleasant valley. A recent clearance of undergrowth has revealed the remains of a small chamber, roughly 3m on a side surrounded by masonry blocks, possibly of limestone. The spring still flows, trickling from a cleft at the base of a thick old ash tree stump, running across the floor of the chamber and passing through a breached wall to empty into a brook a couple of metres away.

The water contains a high concentration of calcium sulphate of use in the treatment of various complaints and even today is said to be used to good effect by some.

St Ann's or Virtuous Well
(Ffynnon Rhinweddol).
OS Map 162. GR 503 051.

The area immediately surrounding the village of Trelleck (Trelech) seems to have been considered important for aeons before the Dark Ages; megaliths are all over the place together with a tumulus or two and other lumps of rock. To reach it, take the B4293 branching south from the A40 at Monmouth town, travel for approximately 8km until you come to the church dedicated to St Nicholas. Go past the church and down a slope to a cross-roads with an information board on the right. Turn left where signposted for Llandogo, travel only a couple of hundred metres and the well (also signposted) is easily accessible close to the roadside on your left.

It is situated in a shallow valley through which runs a small brook fed by several springs. At one time there apparently used to be nine in the vicinity but only a couple still provide water and of these three contain iron salts (good for scurvy and colic). Each spring was alleged to cure a different illness and the once-famous Trelech healing springs were heavily frequented by the sick as well as by religious pilgrims.

The particular spring known as St Ann's has been turned into a well. It is in a pleasant grassy location and the masonry work is well looked after. A recess containing the water also has an offering shelf where people still put lighted candles on holy days thus proving the site still holds significance for some. At one time cups for the use of pilgrims to sample the water were placed on this shelf. The outer surround of the well provides convenient seating for those in no hurry to leave and a neat plaque erected by the local school children as part

St Ann's Well, Treleck

of their "history trail" gives brief details to visitors.

One of the springs - very likely that of St Ann's - used also to be known as a "wishing well". An offering in the guise of a small pebble (preferably white in colour) would be dropped into the water and if nothing happened then the supplicant could go and whistle for the granting of his wish. If, however, a lot of bubbles came to the surface, the wish would be fulfiled as soon as convenient for the activating spirit. Unusually for wishing wells, there was a third possibility - just a few bubbles. In the event of this occurring, it meant that the wish would be granted at some unspecified time in the future. This would naturally tend to enhance the reputation of the well depending upon the life-span and memory-retention ability of the wisher. Since the well chamber is so small it must also have been the practice to retrieve the pebble after use or very soon there would have been hardly any room for water.

A local tale relates how a farmer who once owned the land decided to get rid of the springs for purposes best known to himself. On closing the last one, a wizened gnome appeared before him and peremptorily decreed that if the vandalism was not promptly undone then the underworld would see to it that never again would water flow on his land. The farmer got the message. It's a pity the same underworld procedure wasn't carried out at so many other destroyed wells.

The Trelech springs must be a pretty important place for the underworld considering the "wishing" aspect and belligerent gnomes threatening farmers. It is quietly rumoured that representatives of the fairy variety appear above ground at Midsummer Eve to cavort in the way fairies do, pluck flowers from the field and use them as cups to drink the spring water. The author adamantly declines to verify (or discount) the validity of these reports. Go find out for yourself!

* St Anthony's Well
(Ffynnon Antwn).
OS Map 159. GR 346 099.

From the A48 at Carmarthen take the B4312 to Llansteffan and go through the village to the church of Saint Ystyffan after whom the village is named. It is not advised to take a car any further than this owing to a multitude of double yellow lines followed by a narrow private track.

The well is about a 1.5km walk away and the approach is by no means recommended for the infirm. By the church is a public house called The Sticks. With your back to this building, take the lane straight ahead with the church on your right (an alternative is up a rather steep footpath from the beach car park). When the lane changes to a rough track signposted for the castle carry straight on, go past the castle entrance, over the brow of a hill and past a farm on the left. A little further down the track you will see a bungalow on the right. Take the left-hand gateway here and a few metres on there will be a pair of gates. Again take the one on the left and look out for a doorway in the wall on the right. The well is down a few steps through the door.

St Anthony was Egyptian and generally acknowledged to be the first Christian missionary to Wales. He must have had a rough time of it but he was a survivor - being a hermit may have helped. The plaque on the wall of the well gives his life span from 251-356AD which made him a cool 105 years old when he left this mortal plane to meet the Creator whose Word he passed on to anyone who stood still long enough to listen. He left his name on this well which has been renowned for its healing properties for at least 1400 years (and perhaps very much longer than that during pagan times). Whether he actually came to Llansteffan is not known but it is said that another Welsh hermit assumed the original saint's name and settled down in this little valley to do what hermits do best round about the 6th century when the missionary push was at its height.

The well is in a small and attractive enclosed yard, first walled during the beginning of the 19th century, with the water flow trickling from under a bank. A metal representation of the saint looks across the yard to the small arched recess containing the well which has an "offering" ledge Although the flow is small, the water is cold and bland.

Pilgrims still visit this well for their own secret purposes, the most prevalent of which is for "wishing". Romantic aspirations and reparations are what St Anthony's well is best at, apparently. You must be totally alone, offer a small white stone and wish very sincerely. There are no known statistics regarding the success rate.

* Arthur's Kitchen Well
(Ffynnon Cegin Arthur).
OS Map 115. GR 554 646.

Obviously associated with King Arthur but the other part of the name is a bit of a puzzler. Cegin in Welsh means "kitchen" but he would not have done his own cooking - being a king and all that. Perhaps it was used by Arthur's army kitchen when it camped there for a while - or maybe Arthur was on a strict diet with his own special chef and cooking facilities. It has been suggested that the ancient meaning of the word "ridge" is more appropriate, but that doesn't really fit in with the surroundings. Still, it's the name marked on the Ordnance Survey map, so that's that.

The spring surfaces within a brick-built chamber not quite 2m on a side and roofed over with narrow slate slabs of the type often seen hereabouts wired together to serve as fences surrounding the fields. Two more slabs of this type stand upright close at one side giving the well a slightly Druidic appearance. Used since ancient times it is quite possible that the Druids did utilise this well; probable, even.

Laced with iron salts, it has been used for healing in the very recent past. Sick animals, farm and domestic, have also been cured with water taken from here it is alleged.

The interior chamber is about half a metre deep, the water exiting under a stone kneeling slab to enter a smaller secondary chamber through a pipe before going into the neighbouring pine tree plantation. About 30m to the east is another masonry well-chamber but not much appears to be known about this.

To locate the well, go east along the A4086 from Caernarfon to Llanrug and take the second turning left in the village. Go over the River Seiont and half a kilometre further turn right at the road junction. Nearly a kilometre along you will enter the village of Penisarwaun and must take a left at the crossroads. After another half - kilometre look out for a row of cottages called "Tai Arthur" on the right (there is a nameplate) and turn sharp right into a narrow lane between the houses.

About 400m or so down here you will see the first public footpath sign pointing left down a track. Follow this to the end - not far - and there will be a stone-walled "kissing gate" with a slab of iron sheet serving for the gate. The well is in full view about 40m beyond and easily reached.

* St Baglan's Well
(Ffynnon Faglan).
OS Map 114. GR 460 609.

Yet another important well used for nearly 1,400 years which has been allowed to decline into a state of ruin, more's the pity. At one time a popular venue for those afflicted with eczema, eye problems, rheumatism and warts, it is now less than a poor shadow of its former self. Pins were the usual offerings. Local legend informs us that St Baglan often used to rendezvous with St Cybi by this well to talk about all the local gossip and whatever juicy bits of scandal they picked up on their rounds.

From a rather grand and walled structure with seats and a masonry chamber it has degenerated to a hollow in the ground with stones scattered about the perimeter. One stone still left standing has a scooped hollow in the top and is said to have been used for outdoor baptisms. When it rained the baptism was carried out in the church and water brought from the well instead.

This ceremony was considered so important that applicants had to fast for the 40 days of Lent and the service was performed just before Easter. Puberty was the qualifying age; before this they could only attend the first half of the church service. The timing of the ceremony itself is significant, suggesting that there was some sort of link-up with the old pagan festival of Beltane.

To view the site, the best route is to leave the A478 a few kilometres south of Caernarfon at a place called Bontnewydd. Turn in by the chip shop and follow the lane a couple of kilometres to the first cross-roads in Llanfaglan. Carry straight across for just over another kilometre and you will see an old chapel on the left. This is about as far as a vehicle can be taken; you must walk from here but it is not far and quite a pleasant stroll with a fine view across to the island of Anglesey.

Follow the lane down to Plas Farm and by the first buildings there is a public footpath on the left. It follows a hedge and St Baglan's well will soon be seen a little way into the adjacent field. There is no direct access to the well from the footpath.

Bell Well
(Ffynnon Gloch).
OS Map 146. GR 421 577.

When St Padarn founded his theological centre of learning at Llanbadarn Fawr, Old Nick became furious. Knowing his days of influence in Wales were numbered he decided to pinch the monastery bell and take it to St Davids in the hope that Padarn would accuse that innocent diocese of obtaining a pecuniary advantage in the shape of his precious brass bell and an extremely unholy row would erupt among the church elders.

But he forgot to take along a few muscular demons to do all the hard work and the bell was a lot heavier than he had anticipated. He only managed to fly for a third of the distance when his wings got tired and he was forced to stop for a rest and a drink of water. He set down by a spring on the hill outside the little community of Llanarth.

The spot became mortified as a natural consequence - well it would, wouldn't it? - and it is said that if you stand by the well when the bells in the church only 100m away are calling the faithful to prayer you will not be able to hear them.

What happened to the bell thereafter is not recorded. It could have been a tale concocted by the real thieves or simply mischief-making by supporters of Padarn in his enterprising attempt to outdo St Davids in religious importance - the implication being that Satan had some covert association with the rival firm. Who knows? Perhaps the bell wasn't pinched at all. If it happened today an insurance scam would immediately be suspected.

Even the well itself looks a bit sinister on a dull day. It is a rough masonry chamber set in a hedge and about 2m square. The water is a metre or so below ground level at present and grossly overgrown with weeds. Maybe some historically-conscious person might volunteer to do a bit of a cleaning job before too long.

To find it go south from Aberaeron along the A487 for about 6km to Llanarth and take the first left in the village. A steep, narrow lane will take you up to the church on the right and just past it turn right. Follow the road round a left-hand bend and the entrance to Ffynnon Gloch farm will be on the right. The well can be found a few metres past the farm entrance gate.

* St Bernard's Well
(Ffynnon Brynach?).
OS Map 145. GR 054 280.
Festival day April 7th.

Some refer to this saint as Brynach, others Bernard. If it was truly the latter, he should not be confused with the patron saint of mountain climber and skiers who claims May 28th as a festival day. Whatever the truth, the saint associated with this well started as an Irish priest and later became an abbot of the monastery he founded at Nevern. He was said to have been an absolutely dedicated man who took his missionary zeal to the point of fanatical excess. It got so bad that eventually his wife Corth, one of Brychan Brycheiniog's many daughters, who lived with him at Newport, hired some Celtic hit-men to do away with him. But the job went horribly pear-shaped. Brynach, it seems, was no slouch when it came to a punch-up and ensured his own survival by giving a good bit better than he got. He washed his cuts in a spring thereafter known as Ffynnon Goch (Red Spring).

Nobody is really sure exactly where it is situated but certain "authorities" assert it is Ffynnon Brynach near Henrysmoat where he founded one of his many churches. It's always easy to assert something; the problem then becomes a question of how to justify that assertion in the complete absence of any proof. The fact that the site is on the southern flank of St Bernard's Mountain doesn't help things in the slightest. Still, the spring here will do as well as any.

St Brynach had a large following during the 6th century but does not seem to have been very popular as a person. Animals liked him, though. A pet wolf who guarded his cattle caught the imagination of the locals so much the story was still being told to their ancestors over a millennium later. This tale is also ascribed to St Bernard of mountain rescue fame, to confuse things still further. Brynach may have been a hermit at heart, a bit antisocial, maybe, for he founded his churches and dedicated his wells in places which, in his time, were isolated and sparsely populated.

This one of his wells is now on private ground in a farm of the same name, but a footpath passes through the farmyard (according to the OS map) and the water from the spring can be seen flowing from the downhill side of a barn opposite the farmhouse.

Another of his wells is near the village of Llanboidy on OS Map 145 GR 210 233. An information board in the village car park shows how to get there but it is a long walk. The author was not able to pay a personal visit to this one owing to the steepness of the final approach.

Brynach ended up doing missionary work in Devon where he died in 570AD.

* St Beuno's Well

(Ffynnon Beuno).
Festival day Apr 20th or 21st.
OS Map 123. GR 413 493.

Because three pilgrimages to Bardsey Island were considered equal to one pilgrimage to Rome it was heavily patronised. One of the main pilgrim roads was from Holywell to Bardsey along the coast, hence many wells used for refreshment, dedications and the spontaneous release of religious frenzies line the route. That of St Beuno (pron - very roughly - Bayno), a Welsh abbot who died in 640AD, is one of them; situated on the southern outskirts of the village of Clynnog Fawr. The entrance is on the left just past the Clynnog Hotel when travelling south on the A499 from Caernarfon. It is a couple of hundred metres south of the old cruciform church, which stands on the site of a monastery Beuno founded in 616AD, and surrounded by 2m high walls with seats and steps.

Located right on the roadside, a flight of four stone steps takes you into the walled well enclosure. There are two steps down to the water on each side and a stone seat along each of the side walls with niches above. The fairly deep water is contained within a trough a bit less than 2m on a side. The whole thing measures about 3m x 5m. There is a burial chamber on the coastline several hundred metres to the west which may once have been associated with this well.

This was a prolific healing well if you go by the number of visitors it attracted. At one time there was a belief that stone scrapings from the original chapel columns were good for sore eyes if a pinch was added to a container of the well water and used as an eye wash. So popular was this that the columns were eventually scored with scrapes. Good for warts too, apparently. Sickly children, those who suffered from fits and decrepit adults would immerse themselves in the well during the evening after which they would have to sleep on a tombstone strewn with bracken and rushes for the whole night. If they got a good night's sleep, all would be well with them; if not, no cure would be forthcoming. It goes without saying that a visit to the spring for this purpose would be better taken in high Summer to increase the chances of survival.

One legend states that so holy was Beuno he used to walk across the water to Anglesey in order to preach at Llanddwyn church every Sunday. One day he tripped over a floating log and dropped his book of sermons which promptly sank. Distraught at this serious loss he moped about on the beach for several days before coming across his precious book being guarded by a curlew. He blessed the bird (quite right too) and since that day the curlew's nest has always been one of the most difficult to find,

Heifers with a natural notch in the ear were offered to Beuno at his well - "the mark of Beuno", as it was known. Never one to miss a trick, was old Beuno. Other cattle he had no excuse to claim were ensured of a full and healthy life by sprinkling them with a holly branch which had been immersed in the well water. Clynnog, the first part of the name of the village, is Welsh for holly.

Being right alongside one of the main routes for pilgrims on their way to Ynys Enlli (Bardsey Island), Beuno's well was thus assured of a steady stream of paying guests. Sore feet is a common complaint of pilgrims and a pleasant way of persuading them to travel a few more miles is to immerse them in nice cool spring water. There could have been some dispute about this practice at Beuno's well because a couple of kilometres to the north is another spring in which foot washing was carried out. It is in a field on the right about 100m south of the top of the main road incline from Aberdesach cross-roads. Unnamed and unmarked, but still running today, its use ensured that Beuno's well remained relatively free from pollution by dirty, smelly feet.

St Beuno's Well
(Ffynnon Beuno).
OS Map 116. GR 083 723.

The A55 north Wales coastal express-way has made life a lot easier for traffic negotiating the notorious Rhuallt hill. At the bottom of the hill look out for the sign for Rhuallt then go into the village and follow the B5429 south. After 3km, just after passing through Tremeirchion, watch out for a gravelled lay-by on the left opposite a stone wall. There will be a single house with a pretty cottage garden behind the lay-by. The name of the house is Ffynnon Beuno and the well is in the front garden.

The well chamber is large, big enough to swim in, and about a metre in depth. High stone walls (about 2m) surround it but a good view can be obtained from a track at the side. The original egress for the water has been filled in and the overflow now comes from the mouth of a human visage crudely formed on a rounded boulder. A nicely-preserved hand pump stands by the entrance to the well and a public footpath goes through the garden on the other side.

This spring has definite pagan connections. At the rear of the house up a small valley are caves which would have made a nice home for Stone Age locals and were probably used by holy men after that. St Beuno dedicated the place to himself and a further local connection to this saint is a large, imposing building among the trees halfway between

Tremeirchion and Rhuallt. It is called "St Beuno's" and used as a college for priests.

* Blackstone Well
(Ffynnon Maen Du).
OS map 160. GR 038 297.

At the eastern end of the bridge over the river Usk in Brecon town, take the road heading north and signposted for Cradoc. About a kilometre along this road, climbing a straight hill, you will see a church and cemetery bounded by a masonry wall on the left. Pass this and take the next turning right into a modern housing estate. A bit further, over some humps and round a bend, you will come to the end of the road where it is called *Heol Ffynnon*.

This is the situation at the time of writing. The land beyond is evidently marked for building and what will happen to this ancient well then is anyone's guess.

On reaching the end of the road you will see a gap in the hedge in front of you by a large tree. Go through the gap and look across the field a bit to the left (about eleven o'clock) towards a small sparse grove of trees. This is where the well is located.

Considerable pains have been taken to make this site as attractive as possible despite the depredations of a few slobs who diligently and brainlessly strive to despoil everything they come into contact with. A little pond lined with masonry receives water from a rock-lined chute leading from the well a bit further up the slope. A small masonry structure looking remarkably like a miniature Dutch barn covers the spot where the water issues from the ground. At one side there is an opening to allow an overflow into the chute.

Revered from ancient times, this well is deemed "sacred" though any dedication to a particular saint has not survived. It is a "pin" well where pins were offered to the deity of the well in hopeful anticipation of having illnesses cured, wrongs righted or, in the case of Maen Du well, as an inducement by unattached females of the parish to the spirits to provide a male - any male, probably - as soon as convenient. Just throw in a pin and wish very, very hard - that's all that was required. Nice and simple! The efficacy (or otherwise) of this latter practice has never been satisfactorily proven, for obvious reasons.

Maen Du is Welsh for *Black Stone* and the well's name implies that a sacred monolith or standing stone once stood in the near vicinity.

Whilst in the Brecon area why not go and have a look at a few other interesting wells close by? There's Bishop Gower's well close to the cross-roads and church in the village of Llandew (OS Map 160 GR 055 308), built into an ancient wall. Or maybe visit the recently and very nicely restored village well at Llechfaen (Welsh for "flat stone", OS Map 160 GR 080 284) possibly named for the enormous and very impressive cap-stone covering the primary well-chamber. Then there is the very deep Town Well in Bethel Square in the centre of Brecon shopping centre close to "Boots the Chemist". They're all worth a visit.

Bletherstone Church Well
OS Map 158. GR 071 212.

Although the squat little double-roofed church at Bletherstone is dedicated to St Mary, the well here does not appear to have Mary's name attached to it, though it is reasonable to assume it once may have done.

Bletherstone consists of only a few scattered houses, not enough to be called a small hamlet, and is pretty far off the beaten track too. Only farm lanes serve the area. Perhaps the best way to approach would be to follow the B4331 north off the A40 at Narberth, go through Bethesda and take the second left after 3km from the A40 (signposted to Llawhaden) just before a railway bridge over the road. After passing over a stream turn right then first left where there is a sign pointing to Bletherstone. Just over a kilometre down this narrow lane will bring you to the old church standing on a low knoll to the right.

Just before the church you should notice a small pond on the same side; the well is in the far corner of this. A wooden gate allows access to a small picnic area with tables and an ancient sunken lane leading up to the church gate.

The well is small and only supplies a trickle of water but it is enough to keep the ornamental pond topped-up. It nestles under a bank at the base of a large sycamore tree. A large stone lintel supports other smaller masonry blocks which serve to protect the well chamber from filling with debris eroded from the bank.

The well pool is only about a metre square and not very deep. Water from here was used for baptisms at the church and open-air services sometimes held by the well in suitable summer weather. The water trickles from a mossy slab to the rear and is very cold and clear. On the other side of the pond is another smaller pool on a higher level fed from a sister spring which may also have had some significance before the landscaping works were carried out.

Further along the lane about half a kilometre another "sacred" spring said to have great medical prowess for sick children was regularly used in the past. Unhappily it seems to have been deliberately destroyed like so many others.

St Bridget's Well
(Ffynnon Ffraid).
Festival Day 1st February.
OS Map 145. GR 116 392.

Castell Henllys is a very fine example of an ancient fortified mound (an ancient *Llan*, no less) and has been sensitively preserved by the Pembroke National Park authority. It is an excellent place to take the family for a day out, and maybe a picnic too.

St Bridget (also known as Ffraid or Bride) was born in 450AD and died at the grand old age (in those days) of 75. She was one of the influx of Irish saints to Wales during this period and travelled extensively throughout the Principality lending her name here and there and founding churches and abbeys. She could do things like this because she was an abbess and to make her job a bit easier she took over the powers of Brigantia - the Celtic goddess of fertility.

The great gaping maw of St Bride's Bay in south-west Wales is named after her as well as St Brides village in Glamorgan where she dedicated another well - now apparently gone, though it could be feeding the village pond.

From the village of Eglwyswrw (where a well dedicated to St Mary is apparently being treated with either total indifference or contempt) go west along the A487 for a bit over 2km and look out for a direction sign to Castell Henllys on the right. A lane down here will take you past St Dogmael's church towards the car park and educational reception area. Try not to overdo the panic when you meet the mammoth on a corner of the lane.

An information board contains a map upon which you will see a well marked in the north-west quadrant of this impressive complex of earthwork. There were no JCBs around in those days, remember; it all had to be built the hard way. This well was evidently used to supply the warriors and their camp-followers who were quartered here, but since that time it is said to have been much used for religious purposes. If this is indeed the same spring associated with the chapel of St Bridget which used to stand not very far away (and there is no good reason to suppose it is not) then it would also have been a popular site of pilgrimage. Very little else seems to be known about it.

In spite of this doubt and dearth of information regarding this well, Castell Henllys is certainly an interesting place for amateur historians to visit. There is a small charge for entry.

St Bridget's Well
(Ffynnon Ffraid).
OS Map 116. GR 055 798.

Now seemingly dried up but still in good condition if one discounts the rubbish which has gathered inside the chamber. It is located directly at the roadside just 100m east of the junction for Dyserth on the A547. A low, grey stone wall about 4m long with a small square portal at one end will be seen at the edge of the pavement.

The old parish church dedicated to St Bridget is in the nearby village of Dyserth. It would be a pity not to visit Dyserth waterfall while you are close by and see where another Welsh saint made his home when he decided to go down-market and become a hermit in the 7th century. His name was St Gwyfan, a follower of St Beuno, and it seems he dwelt in a cave under the falls in his old age, there dedicating his own well.

The area has now been landscaped and the well destroyed but in its time it was said to have contained sacred trout which could tell the future by their movements if the right questions were asked (and presumably the right value of offering proffered to the holy man).

The fact of trout being there is hardly surprising as no fish ascending this tributary of the River Clwyd could possibly have navigated the high falls on their way to the spawning gravels. They would have been forced to congregate at the base of this impassable rock barrier in the autumn months. Gwyfan had to make a living and the fish would have provided a convenient means with the help of a little propaganda. This also suggests that the "well" could just a likely have been a pool in the river below the falls. The attractive church adjoining the falls area is dedicated to St Gwyfan whose feast day is June 7th.

Burton Baptismal Well
OS Map 158. GR 055 985.

The village of Burton on the west bank of Milford Haven is in two parts, the church being in the upper section. To find it turn east at the northern end of the toll-bridge carrying the A477 at Pembroke Dock and follow the road down to the Haven then up a hill. Look out for Church Road on the right (the first turning at the top of the hill) and the church is a couple of hundred metres down here.

The well is unmistakable, facing you as you approach the church which is built on several levels with a rather quaint bell tower and sitting on a mound. Between November 1985 and April 1986 the site was carefully refurbished by the Manpower Services Commission acting on behalf of the Presceli District Council.

An excellent job was performed then but the well appears to be rather lacking in basic maintenance today.

Thick water-weed chokes the unusual T-shaped chamber to the extent that the water can hardly be seen. As the well was once regularly used for baptisms it was custom-built for the purpose; the short upright of the "T" providing a set of steps descending to the water chamber which occupies the cross piece - about 2m long and a metre in depth. It appears not to have been used for some considerable time when visited in 1997.

The surround is about 4m square and large enough for a small congregation to stand on the dark slate-covered floor. Steps either side rise to the churchyard above. The walls are about 2m high and the immediate area is nicely landscaped despite the encroachment of that awful water weed.

Just a bit further up the lane is an old village hand-pump fed from the same aquifer which has been restored to a high standard and well worth a look.

Bushel's Well
(Ffynnon Bushel).
OS Map 135. GR 662 933.

Marked (but only just) on the Ordnance Survey map as a small pond, it is nevertheless a spring which at one time was dammed to make a tiny reservoir providing water for the villagers below.

Its only other claim to fame is how it got its name. A certain Thomas Bushel encountered the same problem faced by murderers today; how to get rid of the body. He had performed the foul deed upon his wife, you see. It is likely to have been an unpremeditated murder - either that or he was panicky, drunk or very stupid because he thought the pond would be an ideal place to dispose of the mortal remains of the unfortunate Mrs Bushel. Anyway, he carried her up there and slung her in.

The pool is small and shallow. Mrs Bushel was soon observed to be in occupancy. Mr Bushel paid the ultimate price.

Those wishing to view this dismal little "well" should head north along the A487 from Aberystwyth until the village of Tre'r Ddol is reached. Go past the AA "box" on the right and immediately beyond the next pair of houses on the left (about half a kilometre) turn into a lane leading into the woods. Take the first right off this lane (200m further) and go immediately right again into a wide gravelled area. Bushel's spring is on the right.

Whether due to its history or whatever, it is definitely a sinister little body of dark water. Not at all a good place to go if you're already feeling a bit depressed.

St Catherine's Well
(Ffynnon Cadi).
OS Map 123. GR 498 387.

Not so much a well but a pool in a brook which may have been impounded and walled at some time in the past. It is some way from the source of the brook in the fields above.

The site is within the garden of a house called "Pen-y-Maes" (Top of the Field). If you go up the hill out of Cricieth for just over a kilometre on the B4411 from the junction with the A497 it will be on your left by the roadside.

Originally dedicated to St Catherine (like the parish church) and often referred to as Ffynnon Saint (Saint's Well, which

53

some say used to be near the church but has since been conveniently "lost"), it was subsequently used by the Baptist order who built a chapel alongside over 200 years ago. Wales' most famous politician, Lloyd George, was baptised here.

This chapel has since been converted into a house. Not fenced in at that time, the well was also used by the locals for divining, wishing and assembly. It was especially prized by females of the parish who gathered there during the Easter period to get some idea of their domestic future prospects for the following year. A pin was the usual offering. No medical credits have been discovered for this "well".

St Catwg's Well.
(Ffynnon Gatwg).
OS Map 161. GR 205/181.

From Crickhowell on the A40, cross the quaint bridge over the River Usk, turn left, then right and take the first right in the village of Llangattock. You will see the ancient church of St Catwg built from local red sandstone on your right. Carry along the narrowing road keeping the church directly behind you, past the old rectory (now a hotel) on the right and go up a steep hill then over a canal bridge. Continuing up the hill, take the first turning right (cul-de-sac sign) and the spring is about a 100m along on the left.

A low brick wall supports the outlet pipe which pours directly into a drain. In common with so many other springs of the "holy" type, it is at some distance from the church and up a very steep hill. One wonders why the church was not built closer to the well or a water source found nearer the church but perhaps some form of physical effort may have been considered necessary to acquire the water thus giving it some extra significance; a form of habitual penance, maybe. It can't have been easy for an elderly clergyman in some places on a blazing hot summer day or in the savage grip of winter and this is one of those places. One had to be tough to be a missionary in those days.

No claims of medicinal virtues have been uncovered, though there must have been some, but the water was used in the church font for baptisms.

St. Ceinwen's Well
(Ffynnon Cerrigceinwen).
OS Map 114. GR 423 737.

On the A5 travelling westwards across Anglesey, take the second turning left after the right-hand turn to Llangefni about 11km from the Menai Strait. After a bit over a kilometre, turn into the first right-hand lane and you will find the church of Cerrigceinwen on the right in a little valley a couple of hundred metres down.

Go into the churchyard and follow the path round a left-curving bend until you are beneath the gate you just came through. Ceinwen's well trickles clear and cold from a small rock outcrop in the bank. A plain, simple thing, it nevertheless complements the serene atmosphere of its surroundings perfectly.

Little is known of this 5th century saint. The name is both Welsh and female; in this case that of one of the many daughters of King Brychan of Brecon. Some say her name should be Geinwen but this is a moot point. The well dedicated to her is alleged to possess healing powers to those who truly believe. It has also been regularly used for baptisms.

It is worth visiting this well if only to savour the environment of the neat old church and its tidy lawned yard.

St Celynin's Well

(Ffynnon Gelynin).
OS Map 115. GR 751 738. ✓✓

What a view from here! Just above the tree-line with the rugged fastness of Tal-y-fan at your back and a long-distance panorama over the Conway estuary before you as you stand on the little hump where the church of St Celynin was erected long ago.

When you head south from the fortress town of Conway, take the back lanes for a place called Henryd and you should pick up the signs directing you to Llangelynin Old Church. A journey through narrow lanes, climbing all the way, will eventually bring you to a gate beyond which is a small car park. The Old Church is on a mound to your left.

The gateway into the churchyard is on the other side so it is recommended, especially for those who are a bit infirm, to follow the track out of the car park which is prohibited for cars. Follow the churchyard round until you come to the gate.

It is a wonderful old place, redolent with age, and best visited on a clear sunny day to be able to appreciated the view to its fullest. The church is generally open to the public and is certainly worth visiting for its own sake. It is clean, excellently preserved and services are at present still held there on the third Sundays in May, June, July, August and September at 3.00pm (1500hrs). Don't miss the enigmatic skull and crossbones on the eastern wall.

The well is in a corner of the churchyard wall you passed by on the lane to reach the gate. Once roofed, it is still very presentable and exudes a quiet dignity much in keeping with the surroundings. Measuring about 4m by 2m, it is paved all round and a rough stone seat extends the length of the longer walls. Water is still used for baptisms and is contained in a

St Celynin's Well, near Conway

masonry-lined hollow a bit less than 2m long by a bit more than half a metre wide with a long, worn cap-stone running the full length and slightly overhanging on each side. It is clear and evidently very fresh, as a few outrageously healthy-looking newts testified on a recent visit; lounging about in the water and doing whatever it is newts do when being watched.

This well must have witnessed many a painful and piteous scene in its long history because its primary virtue was believed to be foretelling the probable fate of sick children. A fragment of cloth worn by the child would be placed upon the water, the supplicant fervently hoping that it would float. If it did not, the child would surely die of its illness. The water was also drunk to cure various diseases and used for bathing sick children, these rituals having to be carried out at the first and last light of day. At night, patients unable to walk down the rough track in the dark would be accommodated at a farmhouse close by

A bit further down the bumpy lane leading to the churchyard gate are another couple of wells, one of which (Ffynnon Gwynwy) was supposed to be good for the painless removal of warts. Unfortunately they are hard to find and mostly destroyed in the sacred name of agricultural expediency.

St Cenedlon's Well
(Ffynnon Genedlon).
OS Map 161. GR 482 148

At the northern end of the village of Rockfield on the B4347, about 5km from Monmouth town, the church of St Cenedlon nestles among trees in the entrance to a tributary valley of the River Monnow. Directly opposite the church gate, on the opposite side of a small parking area, stands the well of St Cenedlon.

Little is known of this saint. Sometime during the 6th century she built and lived in a cell where the attractive church dedicated to her now stands. Her well has been altered both by time and the depredations of road excavations but the site has been tastefully preserved in the shape of a masonry structure built into the side of a field.

It is an arched water-shrine with an oval trough and small integral stone seats at each side. A tap now provides the water. The immediate area has many footpaths for pleasant waterside walks.

St Cenydd's Well
(Ffynnon Cenydd).
OS Map 159. GR 427 915.

St Cenydd started life as Wales' answer to Moses, according to legend. Born with a deformed arm and torso he was placed in a wicker basket and shoved into the Loughor estuary on the outgoing tide. The current carried the basket to the peculiar island known as Worm's Head just off Rhosili and cast it ashore.

Somehow or other a deer had come to the island. With the aid of milk from this fortuitous animal he waxed fat and strong until St Illtud took a walk on the island and found him. Illtud took the foundling under his saintly wing and educated Cenydd with the aid of St Cadoc. Reclusive by nature (possibly because of his tortured body) he then went to live on Burry Holmes, a small island at the other end of Rhosili beach where he founded a monastery dedicated to the religious education of other hermit types who needed some sort of CV.

There was no water on the island save what was deposited by rain and collected, but on the mainland close by was a reliable spring near which Cenydd founded a church. Over the sloping village green in the centre of Llangennith at the western end of the Gower peninsula, the Church dedicated to St Cenydd and the King's Head hotel face each other. If you look towards the hotel, the well will be on your left in front of an attractive dwelling called, appropriately enough, Well Cottage.

This is a very ancient well, used for centuries and probably long before St Cenydd arrived. The walls of the original water source are formed of large masonry blocks and covered over with long stones. It is asserted that in the recent past one of these capstones was engraved with a square inside which was a simple cross but this cannot be seen today. Whether this is due to refurbishment (one of the stones being replaced upside down, maybe) or weathering is impossible to say. It is just as likely the pattern may not have been there in the first place.

A few metres downhill the water spouts from a pipe, thence into a drain. As in many other locations, the water was once used for baptismal purposes and no doubt as a cure for certain ills but reliable information regarding the latter function is unavailable at present. The water is sweet and clear.

St Cenydd ended up in Brittany where he died in 587AD.

* **Chapel Well** ✓
(Ffynnon y Capel).
OS Map 124. GR 752 225.

When St Machreth established his church in this out-of-the-way valley to the north of Dolgellau, it seems there wasn't a convenient local spring he could dedicate to himself. So, being of saintly disposition with all the usual abilities which went

with the title, he simply created one - just like that.
At least that's how the story goes. He must have done a good job and forgot to turn off the tap when he left because the spring is still there.

It's an easy one to miss, despite being at the side of a narrow lane because, like several others in this book, it is not precisely where it is marked on the OS map.

At the map position is a little hole in the ground which many would assume to be the dried-out remnant of a well. However, if you go back towards the village for a distance of 100m or so, looking carefully through the hedge on your right, you will find it about 2m from the side of the lane and wonder how you missed it before.

There's not much to see; only a low masonry wall about 3m square covered, at present, with rusty iron sheets evidently placed there for reasons of safety. A barbed-wire fence surrounds the site. A local source reports that steps descend to the water in the near right corner but what it is like under there in the darkness is anybody's guess.

The masonry is not particularly ancient and could date from some time during the 18th century or even later. Good for poor eyes, it was used for medical purpose and baptisms until approximately until the middle of the 19th century.

From the A470 at Dolgellau, take the A494 to Bala and then the first left after half a kilometre. Take the first right up a hill and travel about 5km to the village of Llanmachreth. At the brow of the hill entering the village, turn left around a sharp bend and go to the end of the houses on a narrow lane. The well is about 50m beyond the last of the houses on the left. The ruin of a low masonry wall at the side of the lane has a hollow at one point which was evidently the original access point.

61

Cold Spring

(Ffynnon Oer).
OS Map 135. GR 692 663.

From the village of Pontrhydfendigaid north of the market town of Tregaron, head west a few kilometres along the B4340 to Ystradmeurig where there are the remains of an ancient castle. Turn left here and go about another 3km into Swyddffynnon, once apparently known as Treffynnon (Springtown - or Town of Springs). This makes a lot more sense than the literal translation of the present name which means Office of the Spring. Go through the village, past the old Post Office on the right (at present unoccupied) and nearly to the bottom of the hill. The Cold Well is on the right opposite a house called "Ger y Ffynnon" (Near the Spring).

Within the garden of the house from which the water exits were once several springs which have been gathered together into one outlet. The water trickles from a pipe into a small masonry enclosure at the roadside, easy of access, and thence to the Camddwr Fach brook running close by. It served as the domestic supply for the village and is of excellent quality. Even today people visit here to take away bottles of the water for divers medicinal uses.

It is said that a careful chemical analysis of the water from this spring will show traces of gold in suspension. Be that as it may, don't bother to bring along the kitchen frying pan to do any sifting: it is only a trace and more on the molecular level than in the form of actual nuggets. An interesting point is that Ffynnon Oer is on the same meridian line as the famous Welsh gold mines at Bontddu near Dolgellau and Pumsaint north of Llandeilo. Mystics may wish to read some significance into this fact but it is surely only coincidence.

A couple of kilometres to the north-west is a much more famous well dedicated to the Irish saint Bridget. It is called

Ffynnon Ffraid and is located within the garden of a farm marked on the Ordnance Survey map as Gwenhafdre (OS Map 135 GR 674 672). Actually there are two adjoining farms here and the full name is Gwenhafdre Uchaf. This interesting well is covered by a fair-sized dry-stone building with an arched roof - evidently very old. Although a footpath is shown leading from the lane to the farm it is nonetheless on private property, unfortunately.

St Collwyn's Well (?)
(Ffynnon Gollwyn).
OS Map 170. GR 823 829.

It is believed by a few that this well was named after a saint called Collwyn, but this is considered highly unlikely; the writer can find no other reliable references to such a supposed saint either in the vicinity or elsewhere - he might have been a local bandit for all we know. This in turn casts doubt upon the actual existence of a saint believed to have given his name to Llangollen (the best-known Llan in Wales) where a hypothetical well dedicated to him has conveniently been mislaid. A rather more sensible interpretation is that it is a composite word made from the Welsh words collen and llwyn which stand for "hazel" and "grove" respectively.

Taken with the large number of standing stones and other ancient monuments found locally, this ties in nicely with what is known about the Druids and their sacred groves of oak and hazel - one of these containing a clear, sparkling and reasonably copious spring would be the best of all worlds for their order. It is said to have been used for its healing properties "from time immemorial" up almost to the Second World War, and probably still is.

From Junction 37 on the M4 take the A4229 to Pyle (about 1km). Go through the traffic lights and the church dedicated to St James will be seen on the left a few hundred metres beyond. Stand facing the church and on the right of the graveyard wall will be noticed a paved footpath running into the woods. Follow this path for about 300m until a short line of steps flanked by a handrail is spotted descending to the river on the right. The well is at the bottom of the steps on the east bank of the River Kenfig.

The spring consists of three outlets close together, the largest of which is piped and flows into a small well-trough built of bricks about a metre wide and half as long again. Although the water is clear and sweet, the well itself is not particularly photogenic.

This is a picturesque spot if the visitor can ignore the rubbish dumped all around the first section of the path from the road. An obscure poet apparently called Dafydd Benwyn is alleged to have written some grateful verses in praise of this well after a successful healing visit there in 1580. The extent of his physical or mental afflictions have not been recorded. The Welsh version is in mediaeval vernacular and does not lend itself kindly to literal translation into English. However, it reads approximately thus:-

Dafydd Benwyn a'u cant pan gafas welliant,
David Whitehead composed this when restored to health in 1580.

Duw gwyn i'm benwyn beunydd fo'n nerth
May blessed God be a daily strength to Benwyn
Ef yw naf tragywydd,
He is lord eternal,
Duw ddidwyll da i ddedwydd,
A sincere God for a contented person
Duw'n rhoi fy eniad yn rhydd.
God makes my soul free.

Gan Dduw nef, ond ef, iawn yw dwyn-iddo
To God alone, it is right and proper to offer him
Fe weddi fo addwyn;
A gentle prayer;
Gwelais gael gewdi gloes gwyn
After suffering pain, I saw
Gwelliant wrth Ffynnon Gollwyn.
An improvement by the fountain of Collwyn.

Yn y rhodd Duw gwyn heb gwyno-ffynnon
Blessed God gave the fountain freely as a gift
E'r Ffiniant i'm puro
To successfully make me pure
Iechyd i'm bryd o fewn bro
My face is now apparently healthy
Amylgwyd wrth deml Iago.
In that place near the temple of James.

St Cybi's Well
(Ffynnon Gybi).
Festival day 5th November.
OS Map 171. GR 374 967.

Old Cybi (pron. Cubby) was known as an inveterate gossip and he got around quite a bit, even for a saint. Born in Cornwall at the end of the 5th century, he messed about in the Holy Land and Rome for a while before returning home where he founded a couple of monasteries. But itchy feet cannot remain still for long. Growing restless, he got together with a few other local saints and crossed the Bristol channel heading for Llangybi in Gwent where his acquired habit of monastery building caused another to appear.

From the A449, take the A472 through the town of Usk and turn left immediately across the river bridge. A journey of about 6km will bring you into the village of Llangybi. Just past the church, a narrow and easy-to-miss lane at the side of the village shop will take you to the rear of the church where there is a small paved parking area.

The well is not immediately obvious - even in winter when the vegetation has died back. If you stand facing south on the edge of the parking area (with the church on your right and behind you) and carefully inspect the hedge on the opposite side of the lane you will eventually make out a small solid knoll among the bushes. This is Cybi's first known Welsh well.

Neglected, overgrown and with two wooden stakes holding a sheet of plywood across the well's entrance, it is a mournful sight. The water cannot be seen; only the trickle of an outflow into a ditch behind the hedge, fenced off with barbed wire and cluttered with brambles.

The well-housing is of mouldering masonry, hardly discernible beneath a dense thicket of nettles and brambles. About 1.5m high it has evidently remained hidden for a long time.

One cannot help but wonder why it has been allowed to get in this state. The adjoining church, centuries old, is dedicated to this saint and nicely looked after - yet the saint's well only a few metres away has been effectively and callously ignored. Centuries before the present church was built a chapel stood in the same place - as a direct result of the existence of the "sacred" well. Indeed, without the well the original church would not have been founded in this spot. The very existence of the village itself is due to the presence of the well. What a shame to see it so scorned and ill-treated today.

Perhaps some altruist (there are still some left, so it is rumoured) will adopt and refurbish it one day before it becomes "lost" like so many others.

* St Cybi's Well
(Ffynnon Gybi).
OS Map 146. GR 605 528.

Marked on the map as Ffynnon Wen (White Well), this well is probably more correctly designated to St Cybi. After legging it away from the monastery he built at Llangybi in Gwent he set out to spend a bit of time personally revering St David in west Wales and built a church here on the way (or maybe on the way back). A church wasn't much use without a holy well to go with it in those days so he dedicated the spring close by to himself at the same time.

A bonus for the growing ritualistic evolution of this well was the presence of what might have been a cromlech nearby, now gone. Strongly motivated seekers after renewed health had to attend on the 40th day after Easter, have a good bath then spend the night under the cap-stone of the cromlech. It is likely that this ritual existed right from the initial dedication of the well. How they managed if too many turned up is open to speculation; there is only so much room under any cromlech.

If the invalid managed to enjoy a good night's sleep a cure leading to certain survival was assured. But if the unfortunate sufferer couldn't get any shut-eye then certain demise was imminent; a depressing prospect for a habitual insomniac no matter how deserving and devout. This was also a useful get-out if the hopeful pilgrim was going to perish anyway.

This particular Llangybi is about 6km north-west along the A485 from Lampeter towards Tregaron. Immediately on passing the first houses in the village look out for a little chapel called "Maesyfynnon" on the right by a post-box. Directly opposite is the well. A wooden signpost points the way.

A short flight of steps flanked by a wooden handrail will lead you to a gate through which there is a small enclosure. The well is at the far end under a low bank and the water issues from under a large slab of flagstone. It is only a few centimetres deep, recessed, with another flagstone spanning the outlet to allow kneeling. The water flows into a stream only a few metres away.

There is nothing pretentious about this well but it is a nice little place none the less. Downstream of the kneeling stone a low wall can be seen a few centimetres above the water-line. The depth is greater here and this was probably where the bath-chamber used for total immersion was located. At one time there were seats around for the comfort of visitors who came in large numbers to obtain relief from limb and ocular complaints. It is also said to have been roofed over in its heyday, but there is nothing to support this (both the rumour and the alleged roof).

Dissolved mineral salts in the water actually could have helped certain illnesses, among which were lymph disorders, scurvy caused by the bad diet in olden times and, as always, the ubiquitous rheumatism, though what benefit could accrue to the latter after spending the night under a cold, draughty burial chamber cap-stone is hard to imagine.

* St Cybi's Well
(Ffynnon Gybi).
OS Map 123. GR 427 413.

Designated as an Ancient Monument in the care of CADW, Cybi's biggest well is not one which should be overlooked when passing through north-west Wales.

It is well signposted from the A499 a couple of kilometres south of Llanalhaiarn. On arrival in the village of Llangybi there are a couple of footpaths leading to the well; the easiest passing right by another well (see Feather Shelter Well). From the cross-roads near the church go west 100m towards the school and a public footpath on the right will take you immediately to the one mentioned above. You then turn right through a kissing gate and follow the hedge at the bottom of the field until you see two large ancient stones flanking a narrow opening. Go through here and another 100m will bring you to an old clapper bridge built of large hewn blocks over a brook. Cybi's well is in a small meadow on the other side.

When Cybi decided he had seen enough of Wales he went across to Ireland for a time - then came back for reasons unknown. Landing on a boat somewhere near Pwllheli he soon met up with the biggest landowner on the Lleyn peninsular - the King of Lleyn. This royal worthy was in the process of hunting a stag with hounds. The stag, recognising a soft touch, came to Cybi for sanctuary, which he granted. Thwarted, the King and Cybi came to a characteristic Cybi-type deal, which was this - the hunt could continue as long as Cybi was granted some land to build a church; this area to be within the route taken by stag and hounds until they caught it.

The stag and hounds were only metres apart. Cybi may have put on an expression marking him as the mug of all time. How could the king refuse an offer like this?

He didn't know Cybi.

The saint released the stag which took off like a rocket. The hounds didn't have a chance. All around the Lleyn peninsular they legged it, returning to Cybi who once more took the stag under his protection. The King kept his word.

The large, carefully looked-after structure is in three main sections built from un-mortared and rounded local stones. To the right is a cottage built in the 18th and 19th centuries where sick people who had "taken the waters" would sleep overnight as part of the ritual for a cure. On the left of the cottage are the two wells.

Go to the rear one first as this is where the water emerges from the ground. This is the oldest part of the structure and is almost certainly of pagan origin and later associated with the Druid order long before Cybi arrived on the scene. It is walled on three sides, each about 2m long with the well chamber in the middle. A narrow flagged walkway goes all round and three rough steps descend to the water which comes from under a hefty stone lintel on the far side. This well was used for drinking purposes. The water is fairly deep, crystal clear and cold. On the right it passes under the wall into the second chamber.

This is much bigger and used for bathing. Once more there is a path all around the pool with two flights of steps down to the water. The whole walled room is about 5m by 4m and the bath about 3m by 2m. The present depth is a metre or so.

A small rill takes the overflow under the wall to empty into the brook across the small field. From the door of the big well chamber a rough path made of stone rounded by generations of visitors feet (you wouldn't want to try skate-boarding on this) leads 15m to a small masonry structure built over the rill and about 2m square. The water passes through the rear in a slot in the floor. Welcome to the epitome of up-market mediaeval public conveniences.

The custodians of Cybi's well claimed its waters could cure nearly anything; specialities being blindness, warts, lameness, tumours, rheumatism, etc. For some ailments the sufferer was forced to drink alternately sea water and water from the well for a specified time then sleep in the cottage. All conveniences (including, presumably, the one set a little apart from the main buildings) had to be paid for and a take-away water service was also provided.

Besides its known medicinal properties, the well was used to foretell a lovers' intentions - for females only. On the eve of the pagan festival of Beltane they would visit the well armed with feathers which they would float on the surface of the larger pool. If it floated one way all would be well; if it floated the other way, the false beloved should be dumped as soon as possible. It must be admitted that this custom is said by some to really have taken place at Lletty Plu on the way to Cybi's well (hence the strange name) but that the same divination could be provided at Cybi's with a slice of bread. A similar practice was carried out at very many other wells on the morning of May Day - again for females only. Discrimination was rife in those times but nobody seemed to mind. Each had their own place in life and accepted it as such.

The well being so close to a brook, it is hardly surprising that an eel often used to take up residence, presumably attracted by effluent from the primitive privy just downstream. Naturally, this fortuitous event had to be recognised in the well owner's corporate statement and sacred status was thus bestowed upon the indifferent fish. If the eel coiled about the limbs of a supplicant a cure for whatever ailed them would be guaranteed. Legend has it that a young girl actually died of fright when this happened to her. A whitewash job was immediately cooked up to play down the incident - bad for business, things like that.

This well is still used for the occasional baptism. One was held there in September 1997 and this will doubtless continue in the future.

St Cybi died in 555AD on the island of Holyhead (Caergybi) where he had founded his largest monastery and remained abbot there till the end of his life. He is buried somewhere on Bardsey Island.

* St Cybi's Well
(Ffynnon Gybi).
OS Map 114. GR 401 828.

This one is only included because it is marked on the Ordnance Survey map. The B5112 runs along the top of a ridge at this point and the marked location is a fair distance across the fields. Effectively inaccessible without trespass. Not visited by the author for that reason so its continued existence cannot be confirmed directly.

* St Cynidr's Well
(Ffynnon Gynidr).
Festival Day 27th April.
OS Map 148. GR 164 413.

One of the best-kept wells in Wales - in sharp contrast to the majority allowed to moulder and decay through the vandalism and indifference of the communities to whom they once gave such a vital service. It is alleged to be named after a 6th century saint who had his "patch" many kilometres to the south at Llangynidr on the River Usk. Whether this is truly the case is a matter of conjecture though it would be churlish to object to St Gynidr having a well of his own, wherever it may be, as you will surely agree.

The A438 crosses the River Wye at Glasbury. If you go from here about a kilometre towards Hereford, there will be a turning on the left. Take this and travel a couple of kilometres to the first proper road junction.

St Cynidr's Well, near Glasbury

Turn right and the well is 30m or so away on the left.

Looking at first glance like a rather tasteful open-sided bus shelter with a slate roof and masonry base, a closer inspection will reveal it is in reality a sunken well with an access each side on the front. A step or two will take you down to a flagstone floor each side of the well-chamber with a small wooden seat at the side. The well is a bit over a metre long and a bit less in the other direction. Access is easy as the well is directly on the roadside.

An excellent safety feature - which could so easily be copied at other wells instead of casually vandalising the wall by breaching it to get rid of the pool - is a hinged wooden trap-door covering the chamber with a pair of handles which lift it up to reveal the water. This arrangement also has the advantage of greatly inhibiting the growth of algae and water plants. There is about half a metre depth of water and at the time of visiting there were several coins at the bottom indicating it is still used for wishing.

A neat plaque is mounted at the rear recording the untimely death of one Walter Fenwick de Winton who died on active duty in Africa over 100 years ago. A nice touch is in the few lines at the bottom of the plaque which quotes "Draw water out of the wells of salvation."

This site should not be missed by those wanting to see how a well should really be looked after.

St Cywair's Well ✓
(Ffynnon Gower).
OS Map 125. GR 899 316.

Halfway between Bala and Llanuwchllyn on the south side of Bala lake is the village of Llangower, a halt on the miniature lake railway line. It is here that St Cywair founded a church and consecrated a nearby spring.

Go a bit over a kilometre further west down the B4403 and the road will become very wide at one point. A farm entrance on the left has the sign "Ffynnon Gower" which is the name of the farm on the hillside. There are two springs here, either of which could lay claim to being Cywair's own.

The larger water flow originates in the vicinity of the farmyard but this is some distance from and above the natural track which must have been pretty much on the same course as the present road during the saint's time. The other, much smaller spring, is right by the roadside only a few metres before the farm gate. Taking everything into account, this latter is probably the correct one though it is now hard to see through the hedge and badly neglected.

* St David's Well
(Ffynnon Ddewi).
Festival Day March 1st.
OS Map 170. GR 820 786.

This is probably the best-kept well dedicated to the patron saint of Wales still existing. Born during a tempest on the cliffs outside the Pembrokeshire city which bears his name, St David rose rapidly through church ranks and became a bishop in 540AD. Twenty years later he was promoted to become the first Archbishop in Wales. Such was the religious jollity throughout Wales during his time that local nobles were moved to organise the first Eisteddfodau to keep the peasants happy and creative when they weren't praying.

From Junction 37 on the M4 take the road to Porthcawl. After the second roundabout, carry on for about a kilometre until a cemetery is passed on the left hand side. A couple of hundred metres further, turn right into a narrow road signposted "Moor Lane". After 100m or so another lane will join on the left at a sharp angle. The well is on the right only a few metres down this lane. If you pass under an old railway bridge then you've missed it.

A desultory attempt to restore the well was undertaken just before the Second World War. Before this there was only a muddy hollow cluttered with rounded boulders. In 1962 the National Association of Master Monumental Masons did a nice job of refurbishing this ancient water hole incorporating the original stones. A low-profiled masonry structure was erected over the well-pit and the immediate environs paved over. The site is surrounded with a low wall with a step-over access. A low roof covers the water which is below ground level but direct access to the water is barred by a gate to eliminate accidents. Simple bench seats are provided around the well. It is said a chapel once stood near the well and faint traces of an old thoroughfare can still be discerned leading to the chapel site in the village of Nottage.

It is a quiet, pleasant spot and a commemoration stone now stands alongside the well. It reads thus: "Ffynnon Ddewi. The well gives its name to the ancient dell of Dewiscumbe mentioned in a 12th century grant of William, Earl of Gloucester, to Richard of Cardiff of Nova Villa in Margam."

St David died on March 1st 598AD. If the dates are right then he nearly qualified for a telegram from the Queen, though at least one authority has stated that he lived to 147 years old. Perhaps his daily custom of standing naked, sometimes for hours, in the freezing water of whichever of his wells he happened to be near at the time was the secret of his longevity.

Readers are fervently advised not to copy his example without the express approval of their doctor.

St David's Well
(Ffynnon Ddewi).
OS Map 147. GR 853 529.

There is a bit of doubt about this one, just a little bit. Is it really the well of St David which was associated with the totally ruined church which stood in the ancient graveyard nearby? In the absence of any other suitable candidate it is assumed so. All parameters discovered to date aver this is the case, anyway.

It is lovely water, cool and refreshing and almost certainly the original source of supply for the few houses going to make up the village of Abergwesyn. It issues from a red clay pipe close to the old vicarage, the location itself going a long way towards enhancing its credentials.

From the noted spa town of Llanwrtyd Wells on the A483, turn north alongside the river bridge and follow the lane up the beautifully scenic valley of the upper River Irfon towards its source. A pleasant trip of 8km or so (there are several nice riverside picnic sites en route) will bring you to a road junction at Abergwesyn from where you can gain access to the "High Tops" of the Berwyn mountain range.

Turn left at the junction and a few hundred metres along you will see the old vicarage standing gaunt and austere on the hillside to the right. A little way past this, on the same side, look out for a flow of water falling from a pipe protruding from the bank close to the road at the bottom of a steep field. In summertime it can be difficult to see behind the tall grass but listen for the sound of trickling water. Simple, plain, not photogenic in any way, this is assumed to be St David's Well until proven otherwise. It is worth a visit if only to enjoy the surroundings on the way.

A trip to Abergwesyn is not complete without taking the mountain road west from here up the Devil's Staircase and seeing the spectacular mountain scenery around Llyn Brianne Reservoir. A short distance from St David's well along the lane will bring you to Ffynnon Brodyr (The Brother's Spring) at GR 845 545 on OS Map 147. It is close to a passing place for traffic cut into the mountainside on the right.

Beside this spring two brothers from Abercyncae Farm are said to have fought for possession of a horse during the time of the Crimean War. One died there from his wounds.
There is little to see and the site would not be notable save for the tragic event it witnessed. A small seepage of water has been captured in a shallow trench and diverted into a drain under the lane. The water is clear and laced with some sort of mineral, probably iron, which has discoloured the algae growing there. The writer is informed there once used to be a small, but proper well chamber at the head of the spring, but there is little sign of this today.

* St David's Well
(Ffynnon Ddewi).
OS Map 145. GR 384 529.

Where the A486 to Newquay meets the A487 Cardigan Bay coast road is the major rural cross-roads of Synod Inn. Head along the A487 in the direction of Cardigan town and in 2.5km you will pass over a little brook just before a sharp right-hand corner in the road. Go to the western end of this bridge opposite a bungalow and look over the parapet at one of St David's wells.

There used to be over 30 of his wells mostly scattered over south west Wales but few are left. This one looks as though it won't last for much longer either, unless something is done. It was evidently considered to be very important at one time and the water used for brewing large quantities of booze for consumption at the many local fairs and ale taverns - though this was not its only medicinal virtue.

In the 19th century, John Fenton wrote a description of this well. He stated it was "surrounded by large stones and jutting forth bubbles of fixed air with an immense volume of the finest water". Such is not the state today, due, no doubt, to subsequent widenings of the bridge to accommodate increasingly heavier traffic.

Between the parapet and the remains of an old chamber wall is a wide flight of steps which enable one to get down to the water. A fairly large pool of uncertain depth served for baptisms but no-one would dream of exposing their tender flesh to it today. Leaves, rubbish and water weeds are choking the pool of dead-looking and very unattractive water. This is yet another which could do with a bit of loving care and attention before it joins all the other wells of the patron saint of Wales which have been "lost".

Ffynnon Ddragau
(Well of Tears)
OS Map 159. GR 340 156.

From the A40 by the village of Bancyfelin about 10km west of Carmarthen, turn left into the lane leading to Llangynog. Go through the village and after about half a kilometre you will see a white monument in the shape of a cross on the left. Turn left here and Ffynnon Ddragau is only 100m or so on the left.

More of a spout than a well, and rather untidy. A rough brick wall retains the water which issues from several mis-matched pipes into a drain. Nevertheless, the water is pure and clean and of quite a respectable volume for a spring. A curious feature is the gravity pump powered by the water itself which softly thumps away without ceasing, like a steady heartbeat, sending water uphill through a hosepipe for purposes unknown.

No traditions or stories have so far been identified regarding Ffynnon Ddragau: just a water source, apparently. The well of St Cynog, from which the village gets its name, appears to have been deliberately destroyed quite recently.

* St Decumen's Well
(Ffynnon Ddegyman).
Festival Day November 12th.
OS Map 158. GR 902 021.

St Decumen (Degyman) was a Welsh holy man who left the land of his birth to become a hermit/missionary in Somerset some time during the sixth century. No doubt he led an exemplary religious life but that cut no ice with some of the locals. Unable to make him leave them alone to pursue their traditional, uncomplicated pagan lifestyle, they cut off his head to resolve the dispute once and for all.

But Decumen was a tough cookie who didn't give up that easily. Belatedly deciding not to stay where he evidently was not wanted, he picked up his head and departed with as much dignity as he could muster, leaving behind a spring which still bears his name flowing from the ground where his head fell.

He went down to the coast, hitched a lift on a convenient raft of sticks and floated across the Bristol Channel towards Milford Haven. Once more on his native soil he started inland to some unknown destination. Stopping to rest shortly after leaving the coast (it couldn't have been easy struggling to carry his head all that way) he put his head on the ground and another spring burst forth at the spot.

Where Decumen eventually laid his head to rest, in a manner of speaking, is not definitely known but the spring dedicated to him is still there. So is a pleasant old square-towered church which bears his name and some say that is where he is buried.

To reach St Decumen's well, take the B4230 west from Pembroke town for about 7km and turn off right following a signpost pointing towards the power station and Rhoscrowther (Llandegyman). Go past the power station and oil refinery into the village, past the church and look out for a pair of semi-detached bungalows on the left. A street sign here bears the name "St Degyman".

At present, on the opposite side of the lane from the bungalows, is a deserted farmhouse. The spring is in the middle of the second field behind the farmhouse - about 200m from the lane. A wide hollow in the ground contains a shallow pool 5m or so in diameter with plenty of water weed. There are two water sources; one from a pipe at the head of the pool and the other welling up from beneath on the western side. The water is clear and refreshing.

No verifiable traditions of practices at this site have been uncovered though it was almost certainly used for healing. Healing what, exactly, is not known. Still, the "well" of a saint who was martyred is certain to be more potent than that of the ordinary common-or-garden Christian missionary, isn't it?

Most of the village of Rhoscrowther has been razed in anticipation of an expansion to the huge oil refinery which looms over the low hill to the north. From a sleepy village of nearly fifty inhabited dwellings only six are left. It could come about that St Decumen's "well" may soon be no more unless some determined conservation activity or adoption of the well happens soon.

It is to be hoped that, in the event of further industrial sprawl taking over the area, some attempt will be made to preserve this little visible bit of Welsh legend.

St Decumen would certainly approve.

* St Derfel's Well
(Ffynnon Dderfel).
Feast Day Apr 5th.
OS Map 125. GR 977 372.

At Llandderfel on the B4402 off the B4401 between Corwen and Bala. Approaching from the direction of the river Dee, go past the post office and old vicarage, looking out for a public footpath sign indicating to the left. Follow the path up a slight slope to where a small brook runs under the path through a pipe and strike up the bank on the far side of this brook. A very steep but mercifully short struggle up this slope will bring you to the source at the edge of the woods.

Here is the well, tucked in the lee of a stone wall; a bit ruinous with faint traces of a bathing pool in front. Further down, beyond the footpath, the local farmer uses the water to keep a trough topped up for his cattle. They don't know how lucky they are! They must be the healthiest cattle in Wales.

St Derfel had quite a career. He is said to have been one of Arthur's knights and fought in several battles. Becoming sick of the gore and brutality of the battlefield he laid down his sword and worked his way up to abbot status. Tiring of this he became a hermit in the hamlet which is now named after him and where he founded the church which even today is a place of pilgrimage. An offering there is said to guarantee a pass through the Pearly Gates.

There was once a prophetic legend regarding a wooden horse in Llandderfel church. It used to have a wooden rider with mobile eyes and limbs and was assumed to be an effigy of Derfel in his warrior days. He was often referred to as Derfel Gadarn or Derfel the Mighty. People came daily on pilgrimage to sample the well's alleged healing powers and view the effigy. When Ellis Price of St Asaph came here on Apr 6 1538 he wrote about it and reported 5-600 pilgrims wandering about in the village. Anyone disturbing the effigy would cause a whole forest to be burned down, it was said. The zealous Reformers had scant regard for this silly story.

They took the wooden rider all the way to London where it was broken up and used to burn a Friar at the stake in Smithfield, a place of gross religious barbarism. His outrageous crime was a stubborn insistence that the effigy was capable of performing miracles. Whether it was a coincidence, or down to a certain sense of irony on the part of the London religious authorities, the unfortunate cleric's name just happened to be John Forest - thus fulfilling the prophesy. The views of the stubbornly unrepentant victim regarding the matter were not recorded but he must have been pretty burnt up about it.

Derfel went up in the world and eventually became one of the Abbots of Bardsey Island where he was buried in 560AD.

Retracing your steps from the well, go back to the village road, turn left and a short walk uphill will bring you to the location of the well of another local saint - St Thomas - but unfortunately no trace is left of this today.

Digwg's Spring
(Ffynnon Ddigwg).
OS Map 123. GR 428 507.

Now capped, sealed and surrounded by a fence for safety's sake, this well is notable because it seems to have been inhabited by some strange creature or plant. Fawn-coloured "things" are reported to have been seen beneath the water which may have caused nightmares to spoil the sleep of many a local mediaeval peasant who drank there.
In today's age of calculated reason (don't laugh - there are many who actually believe this to be the case) it is quite likely that someone would spoil the mystery by stating that the "things" are no more than spherical collections of soft algae stained with iron salts.

But surely that is too prosaic for words! Let the well retain its secrets - there are few enough left.

From Caernarfon, southbound on the A499, turn left at Aberdesach cross-roads and follow the lane up to a "T" junction. Turn right and in a couple of hundred metres you will come across the entrance to a farm called "Penarth" on the right. In the first field past this entrance stands a brick structure about 2m on a side out in the pasture. This is said to be Digwg's well. Once a large May tree grew alongside which would bring tempest and destruction if disturbed. It has gone now; nothing apparently happened at the time and nobody ever owned up to its loss.

is named after a south Wales princess who married a common north Wales labourer who had fooled her father into believing he was a man of status. Beginning to worry about the inevitable discovery of his proper station in life, he murdered his wife here at Penarth; doing the dirty deed by cutting off her head and lo, where it fell, the spring burst forth.

The story had a happy ending, though. St Beuno, who had his own and very remunerative well a little way away, just happened to witness the grisly event. He replaced her head (as he did with Winnie at Holywell: good with severed-head jobs, was Beuno) and brought her back into this world. The fate of the labourer is not recorded. Blood from her wound is said to stain the waters which ties in nicely with the story about the algae "things".

This red theme (even the bricks around it today are red) is continued in another tale of the well. Unsubstantiated local rumour asserted it concealed a rich treasure which would only manifest itself to a shepherdess with truly red hair who drank from the well three times on consecutive days in the springtime. Up to now nobody has claimed the prize; there has always been a distinct shortage of carroty shepherdesses around here.

All in all this well has had quite a history. Unfortunately it is now on private land and not approachable for the public as is another possible location higher up the mountainside.

* St Dogeð's Well
(Ffynnon Ddoged).
OS Map 116. GR 805 638.

Go east along the A548 from the centre of Llanrwst in the Conway valley and before you reach the outskirts of town look out for a signpost pointing to the right for Llanddoged. Follow this narrow road for a couple of kilometres and turn right. This lane will take you into the village. Look out for the compact church, of a style unusual in Wales and dedicated to St Doged, on the right.

Just before the church you will see a narrow lane on the left following the churchyard wall. Take this round the back of the church to where a road name-plate at the entrance to a small cul-de-sac says, appropriately enough, Ffynnon Ddoged. The well is the little covered chamber on the right.

Of quite a respectable volume when visited, the water can only be seen flowing in the garden of the house opposite. The chamber is almost flush with ground level and a very small, padlocked wooden door seals the aperture of what used to be the village well long after St Doged (who may also have been a king of sorts) used it. The chamber is just over a metre wide and a bit less than 2m long. A pair of obviously very old and weathered slate capstones cover the chamber. The surrounding area is quite neat and only marred (at present) by a small pile of corrugated roofing sheets placed untidily over half the chamber. There's always someone around quite happy to mess things up for others, isn't there?

* St Dogfan's Well
(Ffynnon Dwgan).
OS Map 125. GR 984 219.

Only included because it is marked on the Ordnance Survey map. It seems to have been neglected, abandoned and even forgotten by all the local people who were asked about it. Being on private land and inaccessible is almost certainly responsible for this state of affairs.

The B4393 runs all around the beautifully wooded Lake Vyrnwy. This great sheet of deep water was created by a great dam which drowned the old village of Llanddwyn. Nearly halfway along the north-east shore a small car park has an information board giving details of this old village, yet strangely enough St Dogfan's well is not marked upon it. From this point go a little further along the lake shore until the trees on the right give way to a series of steep meadows. At the end of the third field a small shed will be seen in a grove of trees about 100m up the hillside. This, it would seem, is the most likely site of the spring which in its time was famous for the cure of ocular complaints.

Little is known of the saint to whom it is dedicated. Even his correct name is a matter of dispute.

* St Dogwel's Well
(Ffynnon Ddygfael).
Festival day June 14.
OS Map 114. GR 351 905.

Anglesey ✓

Followers of St Ddygfael (Dogwel), a Welsh monk and later an abbot, are asserted to still exist in parts of western France today. He died there in 505AD after leaving Wales where he founded a monastery and church in Dyfed. Before that he lived on the island of Anglesey.

About 5km south of Cemaes on the A5025, turn left at the first proper cross-roads and travel east for maybe a couple of kilometres until Llanddygfael Farm is seen on the left. The well is at the rear of the farm on the second (right-hand) bend in the lane leading to a deserted farmhouse.

Water from the spring flows across the lane at this point but you will search for the well in vain. Once very highly regarded for the multitude of ills it cured and heavily patronised, no trace of any well remains. All there is now is an elongated muddy patch, trampled by cattle. After running across the lane the water descends into a ditch. This is one historical well site, still marked on the Ordnance Survey map (assuming the marker dot is in the right place), which will probably never be resurrected - more's the pity - but there is another well, among bushes in marshy ground on the right just off the road, which may be a better candidate.

Dolycoed Spa Well.
(Ffynnon Ddrewllyd).
OS Map 147. GR 872 470.

The community of Llanwrtyd Wells has more than one claim to fame. Besides being the smallest town in Wales, it was once one of the most popular venues for "taking the waters" during the great Spa Era of the 18th and 19th centuries. The first to realise the possibilities in 1732 was a certain Rev. Theophilus Evans, vicar of this parish, who was plagued with numerous ills, including the dreaded scurvy.

Chancing to spy an absurdly healthy toad (some say frog - but what's the difference unless you're a frog or toad?) cavorting in a roadside puddle, he supped from the water to the almost immediate relief of his troubles, or so it seemed. Fired with medicinal zeal, he put the word around. It caught on; capital investment was acquired; bath houses, pump rooms and large hotels were built. Llanwrtyd Wells arose from abject poverty.

Many hotels had their own pump and treatment rooms for the relief of the large numbers of wealthy sufferers who came there to be relieved from the inevitable consequences of their gluttony, lechery and sloth. Most survived to leave again, convinced they were cured and able to resume their over-indulgences as before. Bath-chairs became a common sight in the narrow streets.

The hotel which was built to capitalise on Theophilus' original "well" was the Dol-y-Coed, a large rambling building overlooking the River Irfon (famous for its grayling fishing) a little to the north of the town. Once only a humble farmhouse, it just grew and grew. Every day hundreds of sufferers came to this hotel's famous Spa hopeful of a cure.

If you turn north alongside the river bridge towards Abergwesyn, a matter of half a kilometre will bring you to the hotel on a wide right-hand bend in the road. Go between the river and hotel to a kissing gate and walk along the river bank. This is a popular route called the "Town Walk" and the arched entrance gate to the Spa will be seen on the right. From this arch a level path, quite wide enough for horse-drawn coaches and passing through an avenue of trees, leads to the old pump house and treatment rooms, now apparently unused. The Spa is about 200m from the old hotel.

The outlet from the Spa comes from a pipe 20m from the nearest building to run into the nearby river. At the rear of the complex there is a circular and domed pump room (looking remarkably like a small astronomical observatory) and the water is channelled from its proper source under a thicket of bushes. It will be smelt before it is seen; the distinctive taint of sulphur giving it the Welsh name of Ffynnon Ddrewllyd (Stinking Spring). In the channels can be seen flimsy bunches of pallid hair-like growths formed from a precipitation of the minerals contained in the water. Collectively they resemble nests of thin white worms which would be definitely off-putting to a potential customer of the present day, no matter how ill.

St Dyfan's Well
(Ffynnon Gwyddfaen).
OS Map 159. GR 642 171.

It is strange that the great spring, well and baptismal pond at Llandyfan is not better-known than it is, even by those living relatively close by. The site has had a chequered history and is marked on old small-scale maps as "The Welsh Bath at Llandyfan". First, a potted history.

Dedicated to St Dyfan, a deacon said to be active during the 2nd century (which would quash the claim of the Egyptian, St Anthony, whose well is at Llansteffan, to be the first Christian missionary in Wales), it is sometimes called Ffynnon Gwyddfaen. But this doesn't make much sense to a Welsh-speaker as it could be a reference to both a goose and a stone. Perhaps this latter name could be connected with the Drovers, mentioned later, who also herded noisy gaggles of geese with tarred feet which enabled them to walk long distances.

Be that as it may, it is far too large a spring not to have been associated with pagan practices and its supposed powers would have been greatly accentuated by it also being the source of the River Gwyddfan. Saint Dyfan founded a church there on a rocky knoll above the spring and established his own "patch".

It was a revered site of religious practices for a long time thereafter and eventually a more substantial chapel was erected. By this time the water was in great demand by the sick who came there seeking a cure for numbness and paralytic disorders - among others. There is no doubt that the water does contain strong mineral properties. Many festive occasions were celebrated here and it came to be a favourite spot for playing the games of the time and dancing.

The Baptists founded a mission at the chapel, first using the pond opposite (the original spring) for their rites. This became somewhat difficult later on as the road here became a regular route for Drovers who used the pond as a stopping place to water their animals and also drink themselves silly at the farmhouse next to the chapel which was turned into an inn. It was a busy place at that time; the inn accommodating pilgrims, the sick, Drovers and anyone else who happened to turn up, besides the revels of the local population.

The original village of Llandyfan was in the little valley behind the present church but there is not much left of this save for a few stunted ruins. Still, there were enough people around to form a congregation and it soon became the meeting place of so many denominations it was nicknamed "The Chapel of Mixtures". There were Methodists, Independents, Calvinist Baptists, Unitarians, Arminian Baptists and maybe a few others to boot. The ending of this mix was perhaps inevitable. It seemed there was an almighty bust-up which resulted in everybody picking up their marbles and going away to less abrasive locations.

Then the old chapel was pulled down and the present one built in its place. There are no graves there because of the thinness of the surface soil, yet later Baptists strove to excavate a cavity in the solid bed-rock and created an impressive well-chamber.

Lined with masonry and with a solid flagstone floor, this large, simple construction measures about 4-5m square and a bit less than 2m deep. A flight of 11 steps allows a descent to the water. The clear, cold spring into which they tapped emerges powerfully from its limestone lair in one corner. A wheel-driven sluice gate enables the chamber to be deepened and the water from here was once actually used as a small reservoir and piped to dwelling houses in the vicinity. There are several springs close by but none so copious as St Dyfan's. To reach this interesting site, take the A483 to about halfway between Ammanford and Llandeilo and turn east opposite the College Arms in Derwydd. Follow this road for a couple of kilometres to the first proper junction. Do not be tempted to take the road to Carreg Cennen castle but instead bear right along the main drag. Another kilometre will bring you to the little church on the left.

The "Welsh Bath" is in the churchyard but what will immediately catch the eye is the huge spring erupting into the remains of a pond on the right. Next to the church is the old farmhouse-cum-inn which is a fascinating building in its own right. Even up until well into the 20th century Eisteddfodau, the cultural competitions of Wales, were held in the old barns to the rear.

Attempts are being made at present to obtain support in improving this important spring, tidy the well-chamber and bring the baptismal pond back to its former glory. Being on the edge of an SSSI should increase the motivation for this venture. It is greatly to be hoped that this task, if successful, will be completed in time for the Millennium as a tribute to the long religious connections of Dyfan's spring.

Ffynnon Eidda.
OS Map 124. GR 762 437.

South of the nightmare landscape of Blaenau Ffestiniog, torn and ravaged by the huge slate quarries which once exported their product all over the world, lies the lesser-known but more historic village of Llan Ffestiniog. From here take the B4391 which climbs up and over the "Tops" towards Bala.

After 5km or so bear left on to the B4407 by what used to be the highest petrol station in Wales and follow this road over the moors for nearly 4km until you come to the first left-hand turning to Penmachno. The well is on the junction.

It is unmistakable and in very good condition; the only structure to be seen (if you can ignore a totally unnecessary batch of tastelessly-placed signposts) at this, almost the highest point of the road over the extensive, bleak and windswept peat moors called the Migneint at 480m above sea level.

This lonely well is built of local masonry; a staggered entrance of thick, low walls allowing access to a small paved courtyard in front of the chamber. Rebuilt in 1846, the upper plaque above the well says "Yf a Bydd Ddiolchgar" which translates to "Drink and be Grateful", due no doubt to the scarcity of fresh, drinkable water on this acidic moorland.

The well shelter has a single-sloped roof and is a bit less than 2m on a side. Within, the chamber contains about half a

metre of clear water in which fragments of white shell were noticed on visiting thus indicating some still use it to wish for their heart's desires. It is possible that this well was (and still is) used as a convenient boundary marker between adjoining administrative areas. A nearby and quite unnecessarily intrusive signpost supports this assumption.

As one of the Drover's routes passed by here some entrepreneur decided it would be a good place to build an alehouse. It was called Ty Mynydd Newydd (New Mountain House) but nearly all traces have long since disappeared. Faint signs of the foundations and an occasional roof-tile can still be seen on the level patch of ground to the left (east) of the well.

* St Eilian's Well   Anglesey
(Ffynnon Eilian).
Festival Day 12th, 13th or 14th January.
OS Map 114. GR 466 934.

Rather difficult to get to, which is a pity for such a famous well. Unless you are pretty fit don't try it, and be sure to use footwear with a good grip on the ground especially if it has been raining when you visit here. The best practical approach is as follows.

Ffynnon Eidda, near Llan Ffestiniog

From the port of Amlwch on the north Anglesey coast, go south-east along the A5025 for just over a kilometre from Amlwch roundabout and turn left down a minor road signposted for Llaneilian. Look out for the church on the left set back from the road at the rear of a farm.

On the left of the church gate you will see a stone stile. Go over this, straight through the farmyard (it is a public footpath) and take the wide track leading to the cliffs. There will be a hedge on your left - follow this straight down to the slope (avoiding the mud of another spring) to a stile across the cliff-top path, also on your left. Cross this stile and keep to the path up a slope, over the top and down to the first little cove at sea level a bit over half a kilometre past the first stile (there are other stiles on the way).

Here is a little stream. Don't cross over but look up to your left to where a small waterfall gushes from behind a great rock a few metres upstream. The well is to the left of this.

For a site about which so much is known, it is a terrible shame to see it so neglected. Only a low rectangular wall which once retained the water is left, crumbled and broached at one end. Owing to the small flow of water, this wall was necessary to provide a pool about a metre deep in which ailing people could perform full body immersions. The flow comes from the bottom of a crack splitting a large rock from top to bottom. To the right, against the other rock shielding the waterfall, the remains of a small well-chapel or hermit cell can just about be discerned.

St Eilian is said to have come from Brittany during the sixth century. He is also said to have been a hermit who brought his family with him when he landed by boat in Anglesey. Is this a contradiction or is hermitry compatible with family life, one wonders? Whatever the case, they came ashore in this little cove since known as Porth-yr-Ychan (Harbour of the Oxen) due to the semblance of cow-sized cloven hoof marks found on the rocks nearer the sea. They are said to have been left by Eilian's herd of cattle jumping off the boat but the author has not been able to locate them, however. Perhaps you will have more luck.

The local war-lord did not exactly welcome Eilian with open wallet though, but soon became a convert and allowed him to stay unmolested. So Eilian started doing miracles and things, travelling far afield to spread the Word. All of Anglesey and as far east as Colwyn Bay, where he founded another church besides that at Llaneilian, was his "patch"; quite an achievement in those times when bandits had even less respect for holy men than they do today.

There is no doubt that Eilian was devout, industrious and deserving of having his name recorded in Welsh history. After his death in 543AD his spring was still continually used by pilgrims as it had been for other purposes before his arrival. During the Middle Ages it began to become more commercialised. Much cash changed hands; visitors putting offerings into a chest kept in the church for that purpose. When enough had been collected, a couple of nearby farms were purchased with the proceeds, the rent from these being used to keep the church and Eilian's Cell (now converted into a well-chapel) in reasonable repair. Any cash left over was distributed as alms among the many poor on the island.

Llaneilian became a wealthy parish, though not to the same extent as Holywell where the early custodians of St Winifred's well indulged in the quite blatant ripping-off of a gullible public.

The day before the saint's festival day (whatever it was - the "authorities" don't seem to be able to agree on this) was a popular time to seek a cure or a blessing. After drinking or bathing in the water a prayer would be said in the adjoining chapel and an offering made to the church strong-box. Epilepsy, enlarged neck glands, uncontrollable shaking fits and many other ills would be cured after performing the correct ritual at this time - and handing over the cash. The rule was, no boodle, no cure. Take it or leave it.

Requests for good harvests and curing sick animals would also be granted by whoever handed out the miracles, according to belief. This practice was still being carried out well into the nineteenth century.
The well could not only bless - it could curse, too. Because of a similarity of names, it could have been confused by some with the most dreaded cursing well in Wales; that of St Elian, and the tradition developed from there. Actually, it is almost certain that Eilian and Elian are one and the same. Unfortunately, that called St Elian's well was filled in by the local vicar many years ago because of the notoriety and dread attached to his parish - understandable in the circumstances, from his point of view. Located on private land a little to the north of the church at Llanelian-yn-Rhos outside Colwyn Bay (OS Map 116 GR approximately in the square 86/77), it has since been restored

Of course, St Eilian's well could have been the first to be used for cursing and the one at Colwyn Bay set up at a later date - who is to say for sure? Anyway, at least there is one Welsh well where a good curse can be laid. The way it was done was this. The supplicant would stand in a certain place by the well while the guardian mumbled a few passages of the Scriptures. Then a little of the water would be given to the applicant to drink, the remainder being thrown over his or her head. This would be repeated three times, during which the applicant would mutter curses of any sort towards those against whom he held a grudge or grievance.

A totally different form of cursing ritual is wild-life based. A frog would be skewered with a sharp stick to the ends of which would be attached a fragment of cork. Floated on the well (where people drank!), the cursee would suffer no good until the hapless amphibian finally perished; an obvious example of pagan belief going back far beyond Eilian's time. There were plenty of frogs about then so frog-abuse was quite common.

A more frog-friendly method (or if the curser couldn't get hold of a frog at short notice - or if the guardian of the well just happened to be fresh out of stock) would be to scratch the name of the person to be cursed on a piece of slate or other durable material and put it in the water before making the mandatory cash contribution. If you feel that you really have to use a frog for your malediction, take along one of those ghastly Latex toys that kids seem to love so much and do the dirty on that. They are so lifelike surely no well-deity would turn its proboscis up at such an offering. Half way is better than nothing and times are a bit hard for well spirits just at the moment. Many corks with pins in them were found in the well up to just before the second World War, for what reason is not clear.

This well has seen many strange and cruel things in its long history, which makes it all the more surprising that the keepers of our heritage have allowed it to go so much to ruin. Perhaps it is because of its isolation. It is a perfect candidate for some sort of refurbishment. It needn't take very much - just a few willing volunteers with sandwiches, picks and shovels and a belief in doing the right thing.

On your way back from St Eilian's Well, by the last stile before tackling the steep climb back up to the farm, look around for another little local well. It is shaped like an eye, measuring only half a metre or so along the long axis. Called Ffynnon Llygad (Eye Spring) it is said to be good for (surprise, surprise) - eyes! Small though it is, it has never been known to run dry.

Pistyll Einon
OS Map 146. GR 623 487.

Another example of a well which has been put to modern use. There is little to see other than a small enclosed reservoir with a secondary brick chamber alongside. This is on the right-hand side of the lane just before a farm of the same name. On the left is the original well site, now concealed by a dense thicket and neglected. Traces of what looks like a bath chamber still exist a few metres downhill. It would appear that this is an early attempt at a commercial spa which never really took off. Today, besides supplying the reservoir, it also provides water for a sheep-dip.

Ffynnon (N)Est
OS Map 161. GR 223 182.

From approximately the centre of the small town of Crickhowell on the A40, go up Standard Street for a few hundred metres to where the name changes to Bellfountain Road at the junction with the road to Grwynfechan valley. Just a few metres further up Bellfountain Road, a public footpath is signposted on the right. Cross the stile into the field and quarter across to the right-hand hedge. A matter of 50m more along the hedge will bring you to a footpath leading at an angle downhill. The well is on the left a few metres down this path.

A plain masonry wall supports a narrow trough fed from the rear. The overflow is directly on to the ground in front and has made the area rather boggy. Until very recently this well was very badly overgrown but the local allotment club got together to tidy the place up a bit.

Not known for any other purpose than water supply, this well is worth a visit due to the fact it has been built up for that very reason. It used to supply part of Crickhowell with water, including the old hospital, and is still used to feed a horse trough directly downhill at the end of the houses on Llanwenny Lane and also the allotments 400m away. Its ancient significance, if any, has not survived. With a bit of refurbishment and care it could become one of the many local attractions. The correct name is somewhat obscure.

St Fagan's Well

(Ffynnon Ffagan).
OS Map 171. GR Various - see below.

Four sites have been claimed as being that of St Fagan's well. Quite close together, each is worth a visit. So let us examine each in turn.

Site 1: GR 118 777.
From Junction 33 on the M4 take the A4232 to Cardiff (West) and come off at the second exit at Culverhouse Cross. Take the first exit off the overhead roundabout to Cardiff and straightaway turn left again for St Fagans.

On entering the village (after about 3km) turn left after ascending a short hill past a railway level-crossing and the eastern entrance to the folk museum. Follow this road for just over half a kilometre to the edge of the village and a spring will be seen on the right.

A low wall protects the chamber from traffic on this narrow and heavily-used commuter road. Between the wall and a hedge two small masonry ducts supply water into the chamber. After passing under the road, the brook continues into the grounds of St Fagan's castle and provides the carp ponds with a reliable supply.

The other three sites are within the grounds of the Museum of Welsh life, a display definitely worth a visit. Whole buildings have been painstakingly dismantled from all over Wales and reassembled here in the parkland of St Fagan's castle. When you visit, be sure to allow plenty of time to get around and wear your most comfortable shoes as a lot of walking may be involved to see everything. Now for the remaining three candidates for St Fagan's well which are within the grounds.

Site 2: GR 118 774.
This well, if it ever was one, has now dried up completely. Following your map of the site, head for the old thatched timber barn called Stryt Lydan and stand in front looking towards the carp ponds below. About half way down the grassy slope you will see a curved hollow about 15m across and a tumble of rocks. This is believed by some to be the true site of the well.
It certainly appears to have been such at one time. On one side of the hollow is a small collection of stones from whence water presumably issued before flowing into two chambers and out through a masonry spillway. Provenance is improved by the outline of a building on the floor of the hollow which could easily have been a well chapel. The masonry blocks are crudely dressed and obviously very old.

Site 3: GR 117 771.
Llwyn yr Eos farm was here long before the Museum of Welsh Life was set up. Now a showpiece like the other buildings, it is open to view. In front of the farmhouse you will see quite a large well chamber about 2m by 3m below ground level and fed from a small spring with steps for access. The present masonry retaining the walls is certainly not old enough for this to be the original well of St Fagan and it is suspected that it is simply a domestic supply for the farmhouse. This assumption, of course, could be quite wrong.

Site 4: GR 119 771.
St Fagan's castle is a showpiece in its own right and the gardens are carefully tended for maximum display. On the way to the castle from the Museum entrance you will come to a causeway between two of the carp ponds and just before you step on to this causeway you will notice a little brook flowing under the path at a lower level than the water in the ponds.

Between this brook and the lower pond, to the right of the path, there is a yew tree. The well is on the opposite side of the brook from this tree - but you won't spot it.

Go off the path a few metres and look back - and there is the well, nestling under a low bank and lined with masonry n two sides. It is only about 2m off the path and a metre from the brook. A small pool of water half a metre across lies under a stone lintel and almost immediately trickles into the brook.

Thousands of visitors a year pass right by it, but few will know of its existence unless they know exactly where it is.

Of the four sites listed above, the last, and most insignificant in appearance, is considered by the author to be the authentic well of St Fagan, bishop. it was highly regarded for its healing powers (the speciality being epilepsy) and attracted the sick from far afield. Many returned year after year; not because they necessarily needed to but to ensure prolonged health after being cured of what ailed them before their first visit.

Feather Shelter Well
(Ffynnon Lletty Plu).
OS Map 123. GR 426 411.

The strange title given to this well is open to speculation but as good an explanation as any (given in 1997 - and surely tongue-in-cheek) is that chickens and ducks used to be kept in the adjacent little field and the shelter they were kept in by the well was used for feathering when they were killed. The feathers were sold to the wealthy for bedding

It is often mistaken for the more famous well of St Cybi because one of the footpaths to that site passes right by it.

A couple of kilometres south of Llanalhaiarn on the A499 turn left and follow the signs for St Cybi's well to Llangybi village. Go past the school on the left and head for the old church. Just before the turning left for the church the lane will suddenly become very much wider and a sign for St Cybi's well will be seen on the left. Go through the roadside gate and you will be in a small sloping field just the right size for keeping chickens and ducks, but not much else. Ffynnon Lletty Plu is at the bottom of the slope.

The small and simple well-chamber is set in the hedge on the left the other side of a rather muddy patch. A peculiar standing stone on the edge of the mud over a metre tall suggests a pagan connection - and such may be the case - but the name given to it speaks of a much more mundane use. It is called Carreg Cripio, Welsh for Scratching Rock. This is due to the fact it proves irresistible to cattle and sheep which are regularly observed crooning with delight as they rub their chins, necks, backs and other more unmentionable parts of their anatomy on its surface - a surface worn smooth by generations of satisfied meat-animals.

Taking the water here is said to cure one of the medicinal banes of the time - severe swelling of the lymph glands, otherwise known as scrofula or the King's Evil - and this is also supposed to be the ability of a certain Llewellyn's Well which is supposed to be somewhere in the Llangybi area. The author has not been able to locate this other well so it is quite possible they could be one and the same.

The more grandiose St Cybi's Well is further along the same footpath to the right of Fynnon Lletty Plu.

Five Saints' Wells

(Ffynhonnau Pumsaint).
Shared Festival Day June 29th.
OS Map 146. GR either 663 403 or 420 290.

Once upon a time, in the 5th century, there were five Welsh saints who were also brothers. One would have thought that this unusual circumstance would have resulted in a great deal being known about them, but such is not the case.

Their names were supposed to have been Gwyn, Gwynog, Gwynaro, Celynen and Ceitho. The rest of the folklore surrounding them is a contradictory mess, for want of a better phrase. Two places claim their patronage, Pumsaint (Five Saints) and Llanpumsaint (Parish of the five saints), both small villages in Carmarthenshire.

The sire of this saintly brood is reckoned to be a Roman General by the name of Cunedda Wledig who came to Wales in 400AD. The "Wledig" bit doesn't sound very Italian but it is, apparently. St David is said to be his grandson. A very large proportion of Welsh saints seem to have issued from the fecund and uncontrolled loins of this man and one other who was a south Wales king - Brychan Brycheiniog. Between them they created massive family businesses dealing in sainthoods and could almost be called Welsh Godfathers.

Pumsaint is also known for its gold mines (highly recommended for a visit) which were exploited by the Romans, but at the time these worthy brothers were old enough to start sainting the Romans had left Britain. One story states they lived in caves; the old mine workings would have been ideal for this. Another says they lived together using a communal stone as a pillow when they slept. This stone is on display near the gold mines and the depressions they wore in it by their slumbering heads can be seen, as a nearby plaque states. The problem is that there are only four depressions in the stone - but Gwynaro was always suspected of being a bit light-headed.

Yet another tale relates that the brothers are still sleeping in a cave close to their holy wells. This is again supposed to be at Pumsaint, and the saints will only awaken to continue their missionary work and devotions on the arrival of a particularly holy bishop. His identity is not known.

As regards their five "wells"; in Pumsaint they once ran in the little hollow where their pillow-stone still stands while at Llanpumsaint they were pools in the little River Gwili - a different pool for each of them.
Make whatever you want of these contradictions. The saints certainly lived, they would definitely have had wells or springs dedicated to each of them and two locations claim their presence. Perhaps on your visit to either of these locations you will discover something more factual than the author has. You may even identify one of the wells. If so, please keep it to yourself - either Pumsaint or Llanpumsaint will be the loser and that wouldn't be a very nice thing to happen.

* St George's Well
(Ffynnon Sant Siors or Ffynnon Gegidog).
OS Map 116. GR 986 757.

A strange mixture of pagan and healing practice surrounds this well. What a pity it is on private land and therefore not approachable; the only place it can be viewed from being 100m inside the lodge gates leading to a mansion.

Still, it is notable, and therefore deserving of a mention. Situated to the east of the village of St George, which has a strangely English atmosphere rather than Welsh, the well is part of a noticeable spring-line out in a large meadow belonging to Kinmel Park Hall.

It is a square and fenced open chamber about 4/5m on a side bordered with a few decorative trees and bushes. It has long been used for the cure of sick animals, particularly those of the equestrian persuasion. St George is the patron saint of horses, of course, as everyone knows. It was, and still apparently is, visited for this purpose during the summer months. The old ritual of sprinkling the animal with water from a holly twig to the accompaniment of appropriate prayers is up to the individual. Best practice, though, involved the solemn intonation of the line "The blessing of God and St George be upon you." Being just to the side of the old coaching road which kept to higher ground away from the former coastal; marshes at the mouth of the River Clwyd may have helped to preserve this tradition.

The pagan connection is reinforced by the story that horses were regularly sacrificed here up until at least mediaeval times, mostly by rich folk who thus considered they were insuring the rest of their herds against equestrian diseases.If this is true then it could be a continuation of a much older practice when other living things were also sacrificed.

Including humans, perhaps.

* **St German's Well**
(*Ffynnon Armon*).
Festival Day 31st July.
OS Map 125. GR 193 202.

St German (Garmon, Armon, Harmon - take your pick) was

French and an extremely important figure among the Welsh saints. He came to Wales sometime around 450AD, helped to found a monastery with St Illtud at Llantwit Major in south Wales then went back home leaving Illtud in charge as its first abbot.

But he later returned and travelled all over Wales founding churches, performing miracles and generally upsetting the fiercely parochial Welsh royalty. He had several wells dedicated to him, nearly all lost except for a rather poor thing in Capel Garmon near Betws-y-Coed in north Wales. The best one remaining, however, is closer to the English border.

It is in Llanfechain east of Llanfyllin on the B4393. Approaching from the west you will see a little brick-built hall on the right with a small space for cars. The footpath to the well used to start from here, but even though it is only about 150m distant there is some problem with public access at present and that is why this well has not been personally seen for a proper description to be put here.

Local enquires, however, have revealed that the masonry is still in pretty good shape and a move may possibly be afoot to spruce it up and provide proper access. It is hoped that success will crown the efforts of those involved.

The well is not in the position marked on the Ordnance Survey map which shows it in a bend on the opposite bank of the River Cain from Llanfechain. Pilgrims, the sick and those wishing to obtain water for baptisms at the church of St Garmon in the village would have found it difficult of access in times of flood. It is actually just on the right after passing through a culvert under a disused railway line beside the river.

Giant's Hill Spring
(Ffynnon Rhiw'r Cawr).
OS Map 125. GR 857 148.

The intriguing name of this spring could be due to a certain pattern said to be discernible on the slope of the mountain overlooking Dinas Mawddwy. George Borrow mentioned it in his famous book "Wild Wales". Walking west from Mallwyd where he had spent the night at the Brigands Inn, he looked back and saw a great face - a giant's face - etched on the mountain side.

Unfortunately he says he saw this face on "Pen Dyn" mountain, but no face can be made out here. More than likely he got his mountains mixed up and the face was really on Dinas mountain, now covered with a dense pine plantation which eliminates any possibility of drawing surface features into the semblance of a giant's face. This would make more sense as it is at the base of this latter mountain that the spring which once supplied most of Dinas Mawddwy's water comes to the surface; hence, possibly, the reason for the well's name.

The village of Dinas Mawddwy (good woollen mill here) is just off the A470 trunk road a bit past the centre point between Machynlleth and Dolgellau. Half a kilometre past the woollen mill, travelling north, turn right into the village and go to the "T" junction by the Red Lion pub at the far end. Turn left up the hill and look out for a house on the left called "Tre Mynfa". The spring pours into a small roadside chamber just outside the driveway of this house. There is nothing really special about it but it is a nice little spring to view after a visit to the mill and a good feed in the really pleasant and old-fashioned lounge at the Red Lion.

If you've got sore eyes this was the best local well to visit, it was said. The patient would probably have to dab water on them rather than drink it to obtain relief. The practice at many of these "eye" wells was to apply water to the right eye with the left hand and to the left eye with the right hand. Enthusiastic kick-boxers are permitted to use their feet if they wish - but only on themselves.

A bit further up the hill on the same side there is a small red brick building probably marking the original site of the spring. It is now apparently unused, covered with ivy and the door is locked.

* St Govan's Well
(Ffynnon Gowan).
Festival day probably 20th June.
OS Map 158. GR 967 928.

From the town of Pembroke, travel south along the B4319 for approximately 9km following the signs to Bosherton, noted for its famous lily ponds and coarse fishing. Go through the village and St Govan's chapel and well are less than 2km further. Visitors are advised that the lane to the cliff-top car park is closed at times due to military training activity.

The steps leading down to St Govan's chapel are adjacent to the car park. This is not a descent to be recommended for the infirm or those suffering from cardiac problems though the level walk along the cliff top in either direction provides excellent views of the cliffs and over the sea. It is worth visiting for the scenery alone.

Govan was an Irish abbot, a man of great physical stature and piety who came to this spot to live as a hermit when he retired from doing whatever abbots do. He is said to have personally constructed the original chapel which was rebuilt during the 13th century. He died in 586AD and his mortal remains are buried under the altar.

There are supposed to be a different number of steps leading down to the chapel than there are going up. "Rubbish!" you may cry, smiling in pity at such an inane statement. So try counting them yourself and see if the tally corresponds each way. Most who try come up with different figures. The average is about seventy-three.

The tiny ruined chapel stands in a cleft in the cliff surrounded by spectacular angular rocks. It can be a savage place on a stormy day. What advantages persuaded Govan to settle here are not immediately apparent - but he was a hermit, after all. The cell he called home is at the back of the altar behind a great boulder - grooved, some say, by the involuntary movements of Govan's fingers whilst in the throes of divine contemplation.

A bit further towards the sea is the well, a small simple chamber built over a spring in the prevailing limestone rock. Sadly, no water now flows due to a lowering of the water table, though there is a trickle in some very wet years.

Famed for rejuvenating ageing eyesight, aching limbs and joints mostly, besides many other ills, the waters of this unpretentious well were in great demand at one time and it was a favourite haunt of pilgrims both infirm and religious. Cash offerings to the "priestess" were left on the altar and to obtain the most efficacious cure the water had to be lifted out and drunk from a limpet shell - a mandatory condition. Limbs had to be bathed then the affected joint covered with a paste mixed from a curious reddish clay/soil formed by decaying ironstone found within a few metres. Eyes would be even better than from the waters alone if subjected to a similar poultice. The patient then had to lie around in the sun until the poultice dried out. This still works today, according to rumour. So it should, considering the concentration of iron in the clay (plus the all-important ingredient of faith).

But don't try the last part of the procedure yourself! Observe the jagged rocks below, the spray and undertow generated by the waves, the loose, unweathered boulders obviously fallen from the cliffs above and the almost complete absence of any area large enough to stretch out upon - and be warned.

Only those beyond any hope of restoration will not go away refreshed.

* Grace's Well
(Ffynnon Grasi).
OS Map 123. GR 404 423

A bit less than 3km south of Llanalhaiarn on the A499, turn left into a lane where a signpost directs you to St Cybi's Well. About a kilometre further look out for a pair of sturdy iron gate-posts flanking a driveway on the outside of a right-hand bend. There is a post-box set in the wall. The driveway is a public footpath up to Lake Glasfryn a few hundred metres beyond the gate-posts.

The well is in the north-east corner of the lake and a muddy path leads from the gravelled road at the point it turns away from the lake to go up a hill. It is about 300m along the wooded shore.

At a field gate at the end of the path a standing stone associated with the well can be seen in the field above. The well is only a few metres beyond the gate in a 2 o'clock direction.

It is in a poor state today. A thick surround of about 5m in diameter formed from a collapsed wall contains the remains of a pool of water a bit over a metre wide. The wall has been deliberately breached to lower the water level. The water

111

enters from beneath a large boulder at the far end and the pool is choked with weeds. Close access is barred by a barbed-wire fence.

But who was Grace, after whom the well was named?

Characteristically, several stories have been concocted, mostly variations on a well-worn theme. The following two cover most of the ingredients.

The well-keeper of a village which used to stand on the site was named Grace. One night she forgot to cover the well and it overflowed, flooding the village. The water fairies didn't notice until the level reached the edge of one of their dancing rings - then they stopped the flow. As a punishment they changed poor Grace into a white swan which lived on the lake for 120 years and when the swan died her ghost haunted the lake ever after

The other variation puts the water fairies in a rather different light. The well which Grace was in charge of was only opened when water was being drawn, heavy shutters being kept over the entrance at all other times to keep the water fairies under restraint. It was believed that if ever they escaped then they would creep into the village and ravish the inhabitants as they slept. One wonders how many unexplained conceptions were blamed on the inefficiency of the well-keeper.

Anyway, Grace slipped up and left the lid off. The fairies (who bitterly resented the slur on their collective characters) took the opportunity to flood the village. Grace survived, still living in her hovel at the bottom of the lake. When she died she changed into a salmon which swam the lake for 300 years until caught in a net and given a proper Christian burial.

Both these little stories evolved to explain the regular appearance of Grace's ghost which can still be seen (according to some) wandering the lake environs (or even under the water) bemoaning the consequences of her forgetfulness by means of a lot of crying and sighing with grief. She has been described as a tall lady with "well-modelled" features, large bright eyes and wearing white silk clothing topped by a white velvet bonnet. She is most often seen wandering around at about two in the morning when the air is cold and humid.

(The lake is subject to mists at such times and also the water from the well would probably be warmer than the surrounding air thus creating a column of mist when there is no wind.)

The field above the well is called Cae'r Ladi (Lady's Field) and an ancient stone stands lonely and austere above the well. When viewed from a distance at a certain angle it is said to resemble "a tall woman hurrying along with the wind swelling out her veil and dress". Some time during the 19th century a local wag whitewashed the stone and dressed it in a shawl and bonnet to the great consternation of many. Some people have no respect, do they?

Further legends are mixed up with some bloke called Morgan - but enough of that.

* St Gredifael's Well
(Ffynnon Redifael).
OS Map 114. GR 521 744

Anglesey ✓

Going east from the administrative centre of Anglesey along the B5420 you will come to the cross-roads village of Penmynydd (properly known as Llanredifael). Turn left at the cross-roads and go down the narrow lane for just over a kilometre to the rather over-restored church founded by St Gredifael in the 6th century on the right among trees. Take the left-hand turning here and travel for a further kilometre.

At the bottom of a short but steep hill there will be a large meadow on your left. Over half way along this meadow you will see what remains of poor old Gredifael's pride and joy about 50m from the road.

It is just a sunken hole in the ground now with bits of stone scattered about the circumference. About 5m by 3m and a metre deep, it sometimes contains water and sometimes not, depending on the condition of the underlying water table. No water runs in or out.

It is said to have been capable of curing many illnesses but its strongest point was warts. To get rid of these nasty little skin blemishes you had to use a pin to pierce the wart until blood appeared. Only a little bit of blood was needed - there was no need to tear the thing to bits. The warts would then have to be washed in the well while muttering appropriate prayers and the gory pin cast in on completion.

Due to the benefits of modern medical practice there is no longer any need to visit Gredifael's well for this purpose. Perhaps this is the reason it is hardly used any more (besides being out in a field and on private land). The important thing is - it's still there, thank goodness.

Gumfreston Church Wells
OS Map 158. GR 109 011.

When entering the town of Tenby on the A478, at the bottom of the first steep hill and before the roundabout and railway bridge, turn right onto the B4318. A journey of nearly 3km will bring you to the village of Gumfreston. The road is very narrow through the village so you will have to keep a sharp look-out for a sign on the left directing you to the 13th century church.

A short lane downhill will bring you to the church, very pleasing to the eye and standing in a little wooded coomb cutting into the side of an escarpment. As you enter the churchyard gate the ruin of a very old chapel pre-dating the church moulders in dignified decay on the right. Go past the church door, down a set of ancient weathered steps and the waters are before you.

In fact there are two wells and a spring, the latter trickling from close to the top of a low bank. The wells are lower down; two little pools of a remarkable clarity. These are chalybeate, as opposed to the spring which contains hardly any dissolved iron salts. All are sweet and cold.

The three emissions of water are joined together by stone troughs and exit the churchyard under the south wall only a few metres away. The water in the troughs hardly moves and the levels in all are therefore virtually the same. This emphasises a peculiar difference between the two wells: no matter what angle they are viewed from, the water level in the oval left-hand well always appears to be considerably lower than that in the more circular one on the right. An optical illusion it is almost impossible to reconcile with any certainty.

Streams of clear bubbles, sometimes of quite long duration, continually rise to the surface in both wells - another uncommon feature. The troughs taking the water from the chalybeate springs are lined with a fine buff-coloured growth - an algae of some sort, stained by iron salts - which emphasises the difference in content between them and the open spring.

Gumfreston Wells were once famed for their qualities of healing and each was credited with cures for different ailments from each other. A bent pin seemed to be the most efficacious offering, cast into the water immediately when bubbles appeared for best results. The longer the period of bubbles after casting the pin, the sooner the cure would take place. The best time, apparently, was around the Easter period - especially Easter Monday. The well is still decorated with floral offerings at this time of the year.

A charming custom among local children, also indulged in at other "sacred" wells in this particular neighbourhood, was to carry water from the wells to the homes of local people and scatter droplets over the front door with a holly twig. This was supposed to endow good luck on that household for the rest of the year. Whether the supposedly grateful householder's thanks for this boon was expected to take the form of a cash hand-out (like for carol singing, Guy Fawkes, Hallowe'en, etc) is not clear. Knowing kids, it probably was.

There is a wonderful atmosphere permeating this ancient site below the old grey church and among the dark trees: an air of spiritual well-being and security only the most bitter and hardened will not be able to appreciate. The devout would call it sanctity. If only to experience this increasingly rare state visitors are highly recommended to spend a little time here and to contemplate the relatively superficial "importance" at what is going on in the world out there beyond the churchyard wall. We all need some place where we can renew our sense of perspective at times. Gumfreston church well can provide the perfect environment. It is truly a little gem among wells.

* **St Gwenfaen's Well** ✓ Anglesey
(*Ffynnon Wenfaen*).
OS Map 114. GR 259 754.

At the traffic lights on the A5 in the village of Valley, turn south onto the B4545. After a couple of kilometres you will pass over water at Four Mile Bridge and then take the first turning left signposted for Rhoscolyn. A 4km trip down a narrow lane will bring you to the village. Ignore the first turning left leading to the beach and head for the church which will be in plain view before you.

You will have to walk from here on. A few metres before the church a field gate gives access to a gravel lane leading across an open meadow. Follow this lane for a kilometre to a coastguard look-out station on the cliff top and turn right along a well-worn path. A pleasant walk (on a fine day) of nearly another kilometre will bring you to St Gwenfaen's well immediately on the left of the path.

It is a lovely spot, the area abounding with rabbits and hares. The well is below ground level in a small paved courtyard flanked with masonry bleached by time and salt air; quite an elegant arrangement. In fact, there could be three well chambers, but there are definitely two. The main one is in the sunken courtyard which is about 2m square with unusual triangular flagstone seats in each corner. A set of steps allows access. The well itself is topped by a slab of stone which acts as a sump allowing the water to be on the same level as that in the second chamber outside the courtyard.

Here, a set of four steps either side descend to the water making it easy for pilgrims to wash themselves. The slight flow then passes under a dense gorse bush where the author suspects there may be yet a third chamber.

St Gwenfaen was alleged to be a Welsh saint and one of the comparatively few females to be called thus but there is some suspicion this well may not really be named after a saint at all. "Wen faen" in Welsh means "White stone" and the practice was to cast two small white stones into the pool as an offering for the cure of mental ailments for which the well was famous. Of course it could just as likely be that this practice evolved from the name of a saint to whom the well was dedicated, an association being made with the fact that white quartz stones

117

were once believed to confer magic into water. Probably nobody will ever know for sure which is the truth.

A rather peculiar circumstance is to do with the several other springs nearby. It is not unusual to have multiple water outlets in a small area but look around and see how much ground is above the level of these springs.

There is very little - so where on earth does all the water come from, especially during drought conditions?

Gwenlais Spring
(Ffynnon Gwenlais).
OS Map 159. GR 601 161.

The village of Llandybie stands on the A483 between Ammanford and Llandeilo. Coming from Ammanford, go right through Llandybie and take a left where there is a signpost pointing to Pentregwenlais. Go right through this village as well and a bit less than a kilometre beyond the last houses the spring will down be in a field on your right. It is a little way past the entrance on the right to a farm called Glan Gwenlais.

Although on private land and not approachable at present this spring has an interesting history and was undoubtedly used for pagan practices long before the coming of organised religion. It is the sole source of the Gwenlais Brook and thus almost certainly deemed sacred to an ancient local deity and later seen as a perfect site for consecration.

It has been suggested that the spring was named after some saint who only left his (or her) mark here in the name. What is for certain is that a chapel once occupied the site and was also named Gwenlais Chapel.

Rumour has it that the chapel was actually built over the spring but this is considered unlikely. The volume of water is large by Welsh spring standards and issues from a pair of outlets close together said to represent the fearful eyes of an innocent maiden most foully murdered on this spot long ago.

The underlying rock is limestone - there is a quarry a bit further down the valley - and water has a habit of collecting under this rock, often coming out where a fault-line reaches the surface. This is the case at Ffynnon Gwenlais (and also at Ffynnon Dyfan a few kilometres to the east).

At the head of the spring you will notice a yew tree growing strongly. This tree was recorded as being of a large size nearly 100 years ago and a closer look will reveal that it was cut down at one time and new growth has emerged. From the diameter of the trunk this yew must have been very large indeed.

Even from what little is left it is possible to conjure up a mental picture of how it looked in the past; a lonely valley, a little stone chapel with a proper masonry-lined well for baptisms all overshadowed by a great yew tree. Perhaps this is one which could possibly be opened up for the enjoyment of visitors one day. At present a timber fence surrounding the spring ensures the safety of farm animals.

St Gwnnod's Well
(Ffynnon Wnnod).
OS Map 125. GR 969 445.

Little is known of St Gwnnod but he left his mark on both a church and well in the pretty little village of Llangwm. If you go south-west along the A5 from Cerrigydrudion towards Llangollen, take the second turn on the right over a little hump-back bridge spanning the River Ceirw. Then take the first right a couple of kilometres further and another kilometre will bring you into Llangwm.

Turn left into a lane just before the church and go to the second field gate on the left. On your right will be seen the water running from the sacred well of St Gwnnod. The actual source where Gwnnod used to get his baptismal water is behind a house called "Melisfan" standing among trees on the mountainside. It appears to be on private property so no proper description can be given here, unhappily.

Ffynnon Gwyfil
OS Map 124. GR 618 425.

The village of Garreg seems to have been obsessed at one time with the shape of a bell. Several eccentric stone structures (old refuse depositories or collecting points for the village, apparently) resemble elongated bells and the primary motif of the adjoining estate appears to be bluebell-shaped. This motif also appears on the gate giving access to the source of Ffynnon Gwyfil. The origin of the name is believed to be that of a person.

From Penrhyndeudraeth east of Portmadoc on the A487 (and close to the architectural eccentricity of Portmeirion) take the A4085 north in the direction of Beddgelert. The first village you come to after a couple of kilometres will be Garreg, easily recognisable by the tall bell-shaped tower overlooking the cross-roads. Go past the tower and take the first right (signposted for Croesor) past a quaint old gate-house. In a bit less than a kilometre the well complex will be seen on both the left and right.

The bit on the right is a cleft in the hillside (probably a small quarry) entered by an ornate portico at the roadside. On top is an inverted acorn sculpture (an upside-down bell with an oversized clapper?) and a slate plaque stating the name. On the way to, and just before Ffynnon Gwyfil, you will have passed Plas Brondanw, the local stately home, open to the public and recommended for a visit to admire the complex architecture and clever topiary in the gardens. When stone was being quarried at Ffynnon Gwyfil for construction work at Plas Brondanw a spring which was tapped was put into use as the main domestic supply for the house and gardens.

It can be a bit muddy on a wet day but if you go through the gate into the small quarry and walk almost to the far end you will see an opening in the ground on the left about half a metre square surrounded and partially capped with slate slabs. Underneath is a larger chamber, perhaps a metre deep with a shallow pool on the bottom. This is the original site of the spring which now goes under the lane to the bath opposite. Just before the well will be seen a niche in the wall which once held tools and containers.

At the second section of the well across the lane a semi-circular viewing platform overlooks another well chamber. On one side is a curved flight of steps going down to where it now stands empty. The water at present exits below the chamber in a field except during dry weather. Where the name of this well originated is not known.

Further up the same lane is the village of Croesor and if you are into hill walking it is recommended you pay a visit here for the grand scenery and possibly tackle the path up to the craggy peak of Cnicht (The Knight) which dominates the head of the valley of the River Croesor.

There are another two wells close by, both un-named but interesting. If you turn around and go back towards the main road from Ffynnon Gwyfil, go past the entrance to Plas Brondanw and watch out for a larger quarry on your left just before a large parking area on the right (OS Map 125 GR 615

421). A small bridge parapet marks the spot and a steep, rough path to the left of this will take you up to a viewpoint.

The spring comes from an arched opening in a small structure at the far end of the quarry. It used to also act as a pedestal for a large shell-like plant container now unfortunately broken. The water spills into a narrow water-terrace the width of the quarry then down another step to a pond covering the floor. It is a fascinating place but rather neglected at present, and like Ffynnon Gwyfil it can also be rather dark. The best time to visit the wells would be when the sun has moved sufficiently far around to the west to shine directly into the quarries.

The last spring to be mentioned here is in a bank to one side at the front of the gate-house on the main road (A4085). An ordinary domestic supply, but nicely presented. The Brondanw estate evidently believed in looking after their tenants.

None of these wells have any historical connections, healing properties or stories attached but they may provide a bit of extra interest to well-friendly readers who visit this very picturesque and interesting part of Wales.

St Helen's Well
(Ffynnon Elen).
OS Map 115 GR 484 617.

Researched hints on finding the location of this well were extremely hard to get and somewhat obscure, but by using a process of elimination and utilising the couple of scraps available there is more than a 95% likelihood that the following well is that of St Helen. Anyway, until definite provenance proves that it is not, it will remain the best candidate. All known parameters point in its direction.

So why include it here? Beside being definitely worth a visit, the answer to that is that Helen's name is everywhere to be found around Caernarfon town: Coed Helen, St Helen's Bank, Llwyn Helen, St Helen's Road, Is Helen, Fron Helen - Helen this and Helen that. St Helen once meant a lot around these parts. But ask one of the locals where her dedicated well is and a blank stare will probably be your answer, followed immediately by the familiar words "Sorry, I don't know".

She was said to be married to the boss of the nearby Roman fortress of Segontium (open to the public), a guy known as Maximus, and a warrior in her own right. The famous Welsh Roman Road of Sarn Helen is said to be named after her. Two of the sons she bore him became saints - Constantine and Peblig. The latter founded what may be one of the very first - if not the first - Church-based Llans just outside Caernarfon at Llanbeblig round about the end of the 4th century. On Maximus' death she ruled by herself from the fort of Dinas Emrys. A truly formidable woman of her time.

Being skilled in the art of killing, military strategy and administrative warfare does not necessarily preclude also being highly religious. She was thus beatified, and her well declined in importance. But pilgrims still used it, so did Gypsies and other travellers. It stood at the junction of two important ancient tracks which are still designated as public footpaths to this day. This in itself is a strong indication of authenticity as one of the tracks is the old pilgrim route while the other leads directly to the ancient site of the parish church of Llanbeblig only a bit over half a kilometre away, almost next door to Segontium.

So where is this promising candidate for recognition? Go south from Caernarfon town centre along the A478 to the first roundabout on the outskirts. Turn left to the old bridge over the River Seiont and first left again towards Eryri hospital. In just over 100m the road bears sharply to the right and just a few metres before this bend you will see a small swing gate in the railing on the right. Go through this gate, look along the wall to the left and the well will be seen a few metres away nestling under the paving of a much older road and beneath the roots of a chestnut tree,

It is evidently very old and unkempt at the time of writing, though moves are afoot at present to clear up the surroundings. A low sill retains the water in a chamber roofed with slate slabs and recessed nearly 2m under the road. The opening, nearly a metre square, is tapered in from the top and constructed of large un-mortared masonry blocks. A further interesting, and possibly unique, feature is the row of tall dark slate slabs protecting the opening on one side and part of the front which used to extend right up as far as the gate: the broken stumps can still be seen. To warrant such an amount of embellishment the well must have been very highly regarded at one time. An ordinary domestic water supply would never receive such decoration.

The area is rather muddy so it is recommended you wear waterproof boots. Creeping ivy surrounding the area greatly enhances the definite impression of antiquity and ages of use.

It's just got to be St Helen's well. If you don't agree - prove it's not!

Higgons Well
OS Map 158. GR 962 150.

Once held in high esteem and heavily patronised for its alleged miraculous healing powers in the past, Higgons well has been altered many times to reflect the aesthetics of the day.

The latest in this series of refurbishments has divorced the original well from the public - it is now on private land - but because of its historically local prominence arrangements have been made which allow that same public to sample the water and thereby benefit from any powers it may still possess. If only this attitude were reflected elsewhere for the other springs of Wales now churlishly barred to present-day pilgrims.

The town elders of Haverfordwest on the A40 have co-ooperated with an organisation known as Heartbeat Wales to provide a pleasant walk called the "Trim Trail", here following the ancient path towards Uzmaston church. It is graded to be suitable for sufferers of cardiac problems who are often unable to negotiate the steep inclines and other obstructions so often found on normal public footpaths and is much to be commended. Leading the path right alongside Higgons well with its healing powers is nothing short of a stroke of genius.

It is only 250m or so from the start of this Trim Trail where a small car park has been provided. To get there take the first exit left off the second roundabout as you come into Haverfordwest from the east and then the first right after 50m. Go past the Army centre, under a bridge and the car park is in front of you. A wide metal gate at the far end bears the name of the well.

A broad and fairly level gravel track (not too bad for wheelchairs) leads close to the landscaped bank of the Western Cleddau river and just past the first house you come to is the well on the right. The actual source is up on the bank but the water has been piped to a "Jack and Jill"-type structure designed to act as a drinking fountain. The water is quite OK for drinking and those who wish to imbibe for its alleged curative properties may safely do so.

* St Illog's Well.
(Ffynnon Illog).
OS Map 125. GR 049 232.

Once much frequented for its powers as a healing well for a wide variety of ailments it has today been put to a different use.

Far away from the holiday centres it is nevertheless a pleasant place to visit if only for the beauty of the surrounding scenery both in this quiet little valley and that on the approach roads.

Perhaps the best place to start from would be Lake Vyrnwy. Take the B4393 from the village of Llanddwyn at the base of the dam and travel north-west along the wiggly road through the forest. A 7km trip will bring you to Hirnant.

Here, behind the church dedicated to St Illog, is the old rectory. A short gravel track to the left of the church heads in the right direction. At the gate of the rectory look to your left and you will see a field gate opening on to a steep meadow. There will be a tank with an overflow from it a few metres up the slope which is used to supply the village with water. This is not the true site of Illog's well.

Look straight up the side of the mountain and you will see a small pine plantation with a bit cut out in the bottom left-hand corner. The original well is way up there. Unless you are very fit it might be advisable to wonder if you will be able to reach it even though it cannot be more than 200m distant. The sheer effort of attempting to climb this horrendously steep bank totally defeated the author's calcified arteries and he was forced to wonder how sick folk desirous of a cure would have made it up there at all. A proper description of the actual well cannot be given, therefore. Apologies for that.

But the water from Illog's well is piped down to the tank at the bottom of the slope near the gate and, as everyone knows, the outlet from the well contains all the properties of the original egress itself. The overflow is nice and convenient too.

Unfortunately a large sample of this water (taken amid much gasping and clutching of chest) failed to cure the calcified arteries mentioned above. But perhaps that was because a pin (the usual offering here) could not be found at the time to complete the job properly.

Ilston Well.
OS Map 159. GR 543 894.

From the city of Swansea, proceed westwards along the A4118 on to the Gower peninsula for about 14-15km or so. At the entrance to the village of Parkmill, the Gower Inn (good food here and suitable for families with children) will be seen on your right. Between the inn car park and the Ilston stream alongside, a public footpath gate gives access to a wide level path following the stream. A five-minute walk will bring you to the site which is immediately on the right as you cross the second footbridge.

Ilston is where the first Baptist church in Wales was formed on October 1st 1649 by John Myles (he was only 28 years old at the time). Meetings were held at Ilston parish church (dedicated to St Illtud) until May 29th 1660 when the Baptists were driven out and promptly took over the small and very old pre-Reformation "Trinity Well" chapel dedicated to St Cenydd lower down the valley. Some assert it was St Teilo but there is no good reason why they shouldn't both have been involved - Teilo is said to have died in 560AD and Cenydd in 587AD. An important spring like this could not possibly have been left to remain vacant; even ambitious saints are only human and cannot be expected to miss the main chance. This indicates that the site had local importance for centuries before. Due to unrelenting persecution the Baptists had to leave later in 1660. Shortly thereafter John Myles emigrated to the fledgling United States to continue his religious works in Rehoboth, Massachusetts in 1663.

Little now remains of the expression of Myles' faith. The ruins of his borrowed chapel have been sensitively tidied up and a small monument erected. The main reason for choice of this site by the Baptists was the spring itself which rises from under the chapel floor. Of a copious flow, it was undoubtedly a necessary adjunct to the faith in an area where springs large enough for total immersion are in relatively short supply - most of Gower being composed of porous limestone.

Important though this site may be in the history of the Baptist Church in Wales, it must not be forgotten that they worshipped here for scarcely the blink of an eye compared to the total time this spring has been revered.

This is a beautiful spot in a small quiet vale and easy of access by the able-bodied (wheelchairs will have difficulty in negotiating the unpaved footpath). Sensitive people will recognise by the "vibrations" and atmosphere that here is a place which has been used and respected by folk from countless generations. There is a distinct feeling of sanctuary on a quiet day. The spring itself had, and still has to some of the older populace, an apparently deserved reputation for the curing of sore eyes.

A plaque at the site was first unveiled on 13th June 1928 by Mr Lloyd George of Parliament fame - and who knew everyone's father. It states "To commemorate the foundation in this valley of the first Baptist church in Wales. 1649-60."

* St Issui's Well
(Ffynnon Ishow).
OS Map 161. GR 277 224

Difficult to get to without a car and set in a remote location only approachable through narrow country lanes - even a helicopter would have difficulty finding a place to land here. It is located about 13km north of Abergavenny and 10km north-east of Crickhowell.

It is at Patrishow which is not a village, rather more of a parish centre overseen by the church dedicated to the hermit and martyr St Issui located at this remote spot. When approaching along the last lane, look out for a right-hand hairpin bend at the bottom of a small, pretty vale shadowed by tall pines with the church facing you on approach. On this bend is an area to park the car by the side of a beck known as Nant Mair (Mary Brook). On the other side of the road a few steps alongside the stream will lead you to the well. An interesting feature is the flat stone etched with a Maltese Cross (the Crusader's emblem) at the head of the steps. This is supposed to be the spot where potential recruits for the Crusades were harangued with propaganda and promptly enlisted when their patriotic fervour had reached the required fever pitch.

Some things never change; the innocent and gullible will forever be incapable of learning the lessons of history.

A mere trickle of water within a small covered enclosure is where the well of St Issui issues forth. Yet do not be disappointed at the lack of something more imposing - small is often beautiful and this well was considered highly important in days gone by and much visited by pilgrims and the sick. It is worth noting that the famous ruined abbey of Llanthony is not very far away in an adjacent valley.

St Issui's Well, near Crickhowell

Of benefit to sufferers from a wide variety of diseases, it was claimed. Probably of equal benefit is the location itself - quiet, solemn and steeped in history.

A short distance up an extremely steep hill is the delightful little church dedicated to St Issui the Martyr perched on a relatively level part of the mountainside. Old, walls leaning all shapes and very attractive to the eye, it boasts a small well-kept graveyard and an outdoor pulpit.

This one is a must for well-groupies.

St John's Well
(or Sandford's Well).
OS Map 170. GR 837 774.

From Laleston, west of Bridgend on the A48, turn left on to the A4106 signposted "Porthcawl". At the first roundabout, after about 4km, take the turning left for Newton village and turn left again past the Globe Inn. A few turns will bring you to the village green overlooked by an attractive old church dedicated to St John the Baptist. Take the road to the beach across the village green and the well will be on your left at the end of the open space by the first house.

A small masonry building houses the well and a locked door topped with a grille allows a good view of the interior. One glance will suffice to explain why these safety features are necessary: a flight of steps descends into the gloom, under the earth and far back to where the low water level can barely be seen. It is therefore not accessible for sampling by the public.

Behind the well building at the roadside is a recess within which stands a much later version of bringing water to the surface - a well preserved hand-pump, trough and drain for overflow. This was used before a piped supply was led to the village but the well was in constant use for centuries before that.

Indeed, up to historically recent times, Beltane, the springtime pagan festival, was celebrated here by lighting bonfires. It has been asserted that human sacrifices used to be held here, though this is disputed by some.

St John had an influence over springs to the extent that if running water was drawn from any important spring at midnight on St John's Eve then it would remain fresh for a whole year. This did not apply to this St John's well, strangely enough as running water was stipulated and the Porthcawl well has none, either in or out.

Between the well and the beach is a row of sand dunes several hundred metres wide yet the level of water in the well fluctuates in a regular unsynchronized rhythm, depending upon the height of the tide. The invigorating freshness of the water, apparently, is not affected by this interference of the coastal water table by brine. This peculiarity is said to be noticed on several other Welsh wells and springs - some much too high above and too far from the seashore to be credible, it must be admitted.

But here, the phenomenon has been observed for a long time, a least as far back as 1607 when a poem was written about the well by Sir John Stradling, a noble knight who lived at St Donat's castle several kilometres to the east. A plaque detailing this poem both in the original Latin and the 1610 English translation is attached to one of the well's walls. It reads thus:-

With troublous noise and roaring loud the Severn
Nymph doth cry
New-town on thee; and bearing spite unto the ground
thereby,

Casts up and sends with violence maine drifts of hurtful sands,
The neighbour parts feel equal loss by this her heavy hand;
But on thy little well she laies the weight which she would woo
And faine embrace, as virgin she along the shore doth goe.
Call'd though he be, he lurkes in den, and striveth hard again,
For, ebbe and flow continually by tides they keepe, both twain
Yet diversly: as the Nymph doth rise, the spring doth fall.
Go she back, he com's on, in spite and fight continuall.

Nice, isn't it?

St Justinian's Well
(Ffynnon Stinian).
Festival Days 5th Dec and 23rd Aug.
OS Map 157. GR 723 252

St Justinian, who built a chapel and lived as a hermit on the 253 hectare island of Ramsey (Ynys Dewi), and St David in nearby Menevia were true friends and guardians of each other's life during the 6th century. This is rather surprising because nobody else seems to have liked Justinian in the least. He effectively kept unwanted visitors away from the Island by constantly praying for the causeway to disappear, which eventually came to pass one night to the intense surprise of all - Justinian more than most, probably. Only the ship-wrecking rocky teeth of The Bitches (Ynys Catwr) are left. He was David's confessor which indicates how much they trusted each other.

They had other things in common, too. Neither allowed draft animals to pull carts or a plough to till the fields, for example. Their followers were attached to the yoke instead - while no doubt the pampered oxen sniggered in bovine amusement behind the backs of the grumbling monks. But Justinian took his rabid dislike of his fellow man a bit too far and was so much of a disciplinarian that his servants eventually rebelled. Weeks of severe fasting, group flagellations and other rigorous mortification of the flesh took their toll. Collapse of physical and mental processes became common on the island - the spasms, wild thrashing and rending of garment and flesh being held by Justinian as a landmark on the tortured route to true communion with the Lord.

Things got out of hand. Unable to take normal industrial action against their authoritative master, Justinian's followers and servants did the next best thing to remove their incubus and action followed words in the year of 540AD.

Like poor old St Decumen, St Justinian suffered the ghastly fate of being topped while going about his saintly business. A "sacred" spring arose where his head hit the ground and the spring was thereafter revered for its curative virtues. But Justinian had to prove he was just as tough as Decumen so he picked up his severed head, tucked it under his arm and without further ado left the island and walked across the waters of Ramsey Sound to the mainland. No looking around for a convenient raft of twigs for him.

He had already established a chapel on the cliffs near his usual mainland well and there he was buried when his corpse finally wound down. The place is called St Justinians.

More of a geographical area than a village, St Justinians is at the end of a 3km lane running west from St Davids and it is adequately signposted from there. At the end of the lane is a small car park and a private road extends down to Porthstinian where boat trips to Ramsey Island (now an SSSI) can be arranged. The old priory chapel is directly in front of you as you come onto the private road but it is not open to the public. The well is much closer.

St Justinian's Well, near St Davids

A few metres inside the entrance of the private road on the left is a small well-chamber of the typical Pembrokeshire half-dome shape. It is about a metre and a half on a side with a rounded back and sloping roof. The water within, if any, is inaccessible behind a padlocked wooden door across the opening. There is no water flowing to or from the structure.

St Leonard's Well
OS Map 158. GR 955 081.

This well was earmarked to be restored by the children of the local village school at the time of writing. There is now considerable doubt about this as the school seems to be due for imminent closure, which is a great pity.

The trickle of water it provides is much respected locally, some using it as a source of water uncontaminated by chemicals for the making of wine, home-brew beer (or maybe even moonshine), while others still drink it for medicinal reasons. It is still taken to sick elderly people who sometimes request it to ease the ills cause by old age.

It is just outside the village of Rosemarket in Pembrokeshire. To get there turn where Rosemarket is signposted at Johnston which lies on the A4076 halfway between Haverfordwest and Milford Haven. The church dedicated to St Ismael is on the further edge of the village on the road to Burton and only a few metres downhill from the church a lane leaves the main road off to the left. Go down here to a bridge over a brook and about 100m up the hill on the far side. The well is in a recess in the bank on the left.

Allegedly good for the treatment of eyes, among many other problems, the small volume of water issues from a pipe embedded in a wall of rough masonry shoring up the crumbling bank. Only a couple of metres from the roadside, there is no drain as such and it can be a bit squelchy. There are stepping stones laid on the approach - and see how worn they are by the passage of the feet of countless visitors.

Even though the school may close, one wonders why this should be a good enough reason to abandon the project and deprive the children of the opportunity to do something worthwhile for their community. It is to be hoped that someone can organise something to preserve this little bit of history in spite of very little being known of Leonard. It appears he was the son of one of the Kings of Brittany and was born in Wales where his theological education was overseen by St Illtyd. He is sometimes known as Lunaire.

Little Blacksmith Field Spring
(Ffynnon Caergofaint Fach).
OS Map 123 GR 442 531.

Not so long ago it is said that a family suffering from extreme poverty lived in a hovel close beside the coast road south of Caernarfon. It was one of the main Drover routes, besides being one of the pilgrim paths to Ynys Enlli.

Such a desperate state of financial need can nearly always be put down to one of three basic causes: gross laziness, inordinate bad luck or true honesty. For this particular family the last was the reason for their impoverishment. The father, slaving away in a poorly-paid and insecure job as a road-stone cutter, only made things worse due to his total ignorance of sensible family planning.

In spite of their financial devastation, when an old gipsy woman in obviously worse straits than themselves knocked on their door, they managed to scrape together a few coins to buy a small posy of dried flowers they didn't need from her meagre stock of wares. In parting, she told them that fortune would be theirs one day as a reward for their kindness.

Things got no better yet the poor family always gave succour to others when needed. One day a landau carrying wealthy pilgrims to Ynys Enlli stopped by their door beseeching warm water for one of their number who looked like he wasn't going to make it anywhere near to the Isle of Saints. Water was taken from the well, boiled, and used to successfully revive the invalid. The pilgrims were given shelter for the night and fed the sparse rations which should have gone to the children. In the morning the landau left.

Going to the well for water for the day, the mother of the family found a draw-string pouch full of gold coins and jewellery on the cap-stone. Strenuous efforts were made to find the pilgrims to no avail. After some years, during which not a penny of the treasure was touched, they were finally prevailed upon by friends to view the wealth as a gift for their generosity. They bought a farm and, accustomed to hard work, prospered greatly.

The well they used is very old and was patronised by pilgrims, drovers and gypsies. It is still being used for domestic uses despite its small size and volume. Purple slate forms the cap-stone, sill and top edging, below which is a much older construction of rounded boulders. The water passes through a small, neat chamber hardly 70cm x 60cm in size and 25cm in depth. It is cold and bland with no special claims for miracle cures.

To find it you must go south along the A499 from Caernarfon towards Pwllheli for about 15km to the village of Pontllyfni and take the only turning right in the village by the river bridge. Keep close to the river Llyfni for about a kilometre until you reach the ancient and narrow pack-horse bridge of

Pont-y-Cim, built in 1612 after a local tragedy and complete with resident ghost. Just over the bridge take the left fork and travel along a narrow, winding lane for another kilometre to the first bit of downhill slope. Ffynnon Caergofaint Bach is halfway down the little hill on the right, tucked tightly into the bank under a thick hedge of blackthorn and ivy. All that remains of the old cottage can be seen uphill of the well on the same side.

Llandaff Village Well
OS Map 171. GR 155 777.

Worthy of note because it is one of the few Welsh wells used for domestic village purposes which has been preserved in its original form. It is about 2m long and just over a metre in width. The arched opening from which water used to be drawn has been sealed for safety and there are two rather interesting niches in the outside wall facing the road. What purpose they serve is obscure; they could simply be ornamental or maybe something to do with the washing of cheeses here by the local dairy women.

From the High Street in Llandaff, Cardiff, turn down the main road (A4119) in the direction of the city centre by the Black Lion public house and walk about 40m to the well. It is tucked away in a corner of the pavement just past the old Registry building. Traffic ceaselessly thunders by on this busy artery, to and from Cardiff, never-ending. How much different it must have been in the days when local people used to gather there to draw their water supplies and exchange gossip. It is more than a world away in both time and pace of life.

The well is now dry, like St Teilo's around the corner; a natural consequence of the massive increase in the number of houses in this Victorian suburb.

Llandeloy Church Well
OS Map 157. GR 856 266.

A large tract of the western part of Pembrokeshire is a gently-undulating plateau of rich agricultural land not particularly rich in watercourses. It is the sort of water-sparse environment one does not expect to find a spring of quite reasonable flow, especially at a spot which does not have a great deal of higher ground to draw from.

Indisputably endowed with pagan connections, it was almost certainly the only reason for the little church being established at Llandeloy. The flow forms a minor tributary of the River Solva so it is not too surprising to hear that "sacred fish" - probably eels - took up residence at the spring-head.

The well consists of two connected hollows, most of the water rising in the smaller one. With a maximum depth of 30cm, the total area covered is about 4-5m in length by 1-2m in width. Occasional bursts of bubbles rise in the smaller chamber which would probably have been looked upon as incontrovertible proof of an inhabited underworld in ancient times.

A surge of current can be seen disturbing the surface of the smaller pool, the exit point being beneath a crude step. Undressed masonry blocks surround both pools, the sad remains of what was once a proper bathing chamber quite big enough to be used for total body baptisms. Little is known of any medicinal powers. Destruction of the retaining walls has resulted in the water level being greatly diminished and it is now led away by a straight ditch.

This is a perfect site for restoration and is certainly worth a visit if you are in the vicinity. It can be a bit tricky to find, though.

The easiest way, perhaps, would be to go west from Haverfordwest along the A487 St Davids road to the great storm beach at Newgale. Ascend the steep hill on the other side of the bay and turn right at the top. Follow this road alongside Brawdy airfield until you pick up the signs for Llandeloy. When you reach the village go past the post office looking out for Ivy Cottage on the inside of a right-hand bend.

A path on the left will take you to the church a few metres away. Go to the opposite side of the church, continue in the same direction and the well is in front of a tangled hedgerow at the far side of the churchyard.

Llangammarch Spa Well
OS Map 147. GR 945 476.

Going west along the A483 from Builth Wells, just after the village of Garth, turn left for Llangammarch Wells. You will reach the village after 4-5km. Just after the railway station, go left under the railway bridge, over the river and left again at the post office. Follow this lane for just over a kilometre until you come to a dip immediately before the Lake County Hotel entrance. At the bottom of the dip you will see a swing-gate on the left by the side of a brook. Go through this gate and the well is about 70m away by the river bank.

Once a favoured resort for royalty and VIPs from all over the world, the red-brick bath-house is about 7m square with a small walled masonry verandah to one side and what appears to be a open-air bath chamber on the other. Hundreds came here, thronging the immediate area and often holding wild spontaneous parties for their many guests.

It is now in a shocking state. The roof has fallen in; heavy timbers lying scattered where they landed. The original marble lining has been stripped from the bath chambers and weeds abound.

The springs, mostly sulphur and bromide, have virtually dried up, only a seepage sometimes being observed from time to time after sustained rainfall. This once-famous well, the sole reason for the existence of the village, is now a historical disaster area, collapsing and decaying.

In the opposite side of the field by the river bank a bridge over the brook will lead you away from this scene of hideous neglect on to a level pathway which follows the River Irfon back to the village. It is an extremely pleasant 1.5km walk which will help to put what you have just seen out of your mind.

* Llanychaer Well
(Ffynnon Sant or Ffynnon Llanllawer).
OS Map 157. GR 986 360.

The only "cursing" well known to still exist in south Wales. If you want to feel you are getting some sort of revenge on your works manager or any other natural enemy this is the place to come. Make sure you take along a pin to bend while you make the curse then throw it into the well. Managers can also use it to curse their staff.

But at the time of writing you may have a bit of difficulty in finding enough water to cover the pin, bent or not. This is due to pipeline works being carried out in an adjoining field only a few metres away. Hopefully the contractors will ensure that the well once more receives enough water to keep it in the condition it has enjoyed for a few thousand years when they finish. Anything less would be simple, crass vandalism. St Eilian's well in Anglesey can then be consulted to thoroughly curse the contractors.

It used to be renowned for curing many disorders - so much so that it was regarded as a truly miraculous place. Repairing painful and failing eyes was the speciality it is said and an unbent pin was the usual payment for this type of request. The water was regularly used for baptisms and indeed the chamber itself is quite large enough for full body immersion. The trouble is that it may have involved stooping in the present structure which is only a couple of metres high and in the shape of an arch.

Of course, the building itself is relatively recent as far as the using of this well is concerned. It is about 2m wide and nearly 3m long. Constructed in the usual Pembrokeshire half-crash helmet manner, it now has a wooden gate across the front. In ancient times baptism would have been a lot more convenient with an open top.

The church and well are on high ground overlooking the beautiful Gwaun valley just outside Fishguard. An exploratory tour of this valley and the enclosing hills is highly recommended despite the many steep hills.

To find the well go along the B4313 east from Fishguard upper town for just over 3km to Llanychaer and turn left past the public house. Over the river bridge turn left again and a very steep hill will take you up to the church standing on a mound to the left at the top. A house called Glan Ffynnon is on the same side as the church and the well is in a field at the rear of the house, hidden by a hedge. There is a signpost stating "Ffynnon Llanllawer" and the well is only a few metres beyond the gate.

Llanchaer, near Fishguard

St Llawddog's Well
(Ffynnon Llawddog).
Festival Day 15th January.
OS Map 145. GR 268 416.

The little village of Cenarth on the River Teifi is a popular place for visitors drawn there by the splendid waterfall and deep pools where coracle fishermen can still be observed plying their ancient art. Fishing for the noble Teifi salmon can be obtained here.

At one end of the old bridge, built in the typical Teifi Valley architectural style, the B4332 branches off from the A484 and only a few metres down this minor road the well can be seen on the right, on the river bank.

Dedicated to the Welsh confessor St Llawddog in the 6th century, like the village church, it has recently been reconstructed to a high standard. It is good to see a community which respects its heritage. Approximately a couple of metres on a side, the square well housing sports a double-pitched roof of thick slate slabs. On each end is a slate plaque nicely etched with a cross and the well's name. A cobblestone path surrounds the site.

On the side facing the river is an outlet pipe from which trickles a small water flow. It is fresh, yet bland, and once had a good reputation for the cure of various ailments far into the 19th century.

Lluan Chapel Well
(Ffynnon Capel Lluan).
OS Map 159. GR 555 183.

When travelling through the high places of Wales one often comes across lonely old chapels, often only used once or twice

St Llawddog's Well, Cenarth

a year (if at all) which are gradually crumbling and blending into their surroundings. Most are used by an Independent order while others are in ruins or just a memory. Rarely do they have any kind of associated spring.

But others, mostly those on an ancient Catholic site, do. Examples would be Capel Llugwy in Anglesey or Capel Dewi in the foothills of the Black Mountain. Being on high ground, their springs have nearly all dried up these days due to a general lowering of the water table.

Capel Lluan spring is one of those rare exceptions. If you leave the A48 at Crosshands roundabout and follow the A476 north in the direction of Llandeilo, a trip of 3km will bring you to the junction of the B4297 on the left. Turn here and travel 4km to the hamlet of Penrhiwgoch. At the far end of the few houses you will see a large farm on the right called Garngoch and then there will be a right-hand bend. On the outside of this bend (to the left) there is a small, hard-to-see kissing gate giving access to a public footpath.

Through the gate, follow the ditch on the left for about 150m and you will find a straight fenced rill which cuts across the field. At the top end of this there is a little spring, evidently of the chalybeate variety judging by the colour. This is said to be the site of Ffynnon Lluan but only very faint, and probably imaginary traces of a proper well chamber can be made out, the channel having been straightened for land drainage purposes.

Beyond the spring, about 30m distant, a dark shape and a few tombstones can be espied through a scattering of small trees and bushes. This is the ruinous remains of the old Capel Lluan which is known to some as the Chapel of the Owls, for reasons obscure. Maybe the name is a corruption of the Welsh word for "owl" but chances are that there really was a St Lluan only remembered by the name of this sad ruin.

Yet it is a pleasant spot with overtones of melancholy, this little place which was once much frequented for sincere worship. Not much has been discovered about the history or that of the spring though its waters were said to be used for baptisms at the font in the chapel.

* Margaret's Well
(Ffynnon Farged).
OS Map 158. GR 111 118.

From the A44 near Narberth, take the A478 south towards Tenby and after about 8km you will enter the village of Templeton. The B4315 will join on the left and directly opposite is a lane. Go up this lane a matter of 30m and a narrower single-track lane will be on your left. Only a few paces along this lane you will see a footpath sign and a small swing gate on the left.

Follow the tree-lined path for about 200m until you come to a steeper part and the well will be immediately around the corner on the right. It still provides a flow of water despite recent building developments in the village close by. A small and very basic masonry structure houses the well which overflows into a shallow pool.

Little is known about Margaret after whom the well is named; possibly one of the St Margarets or a local healing woman who looked after it. The site is evidently reasonably cared-for.

St Mary's Well
(Ffynnon Fair).
OS Map 124. GR 581 311.

St Mary, mother of Jesus, was the main standby of Catholic missionaries who were too self-conscious to append their own names to the parishes they carved from the Welsh religious wilderness. A few centuries after the Age of Saints there was another rush of dedications in her name. As a result there are over 60 churches dedicated to her in Wales and more wells in her name than any other saint. Most of them have been destroyed or lost in the couldn't-care-less interval between then and now.

But a few still remain. One of them is in Harlech close to the mighty fortress which is thronged with tourists in the season. How many of them, one wonders, know about the ancient and sacred parish spring so close at hand?

Unhappily, like so many others, it is now ignored; overshadowed by the more grandiose ruins of the castle. The fact it was being revered for hundreds of years before the castle was built doesn't seen to count for much these days. Yet it is only a matter of 3m outside the castle walls. Surely the castle custodians could give it a bit more status!

Just before you reach the ticket office to enter the castle grounds go through a littler gate on the right into a grassy children's play area. Keep to the left and look over the fence directly behind the ticket and information office. The water will be heard before it is seen - the spring is quite substantial. It flows in a gully from under the playground to tumble down the steep hillside and was once used to power an old mill, now a private house. It seems this water-course is now also used as an exit for some of the rain gullies in the High Street.

It doesn't look much now, but imagine how the surroundings must have been when the well was dedicated - long, so long before the castle was erected. A bare, craggy and windswept cliff overlooking the sea with the waves pounding directly below. Even after the castle was put there the sea came right up to the foot of the cliff, covering where the railway station now stands. It must have been a setting of great grandeur and quite appropriate for the sacred well of the central parish of Llanfair a little further south on the coast.

St Mary's Well
(Ffynnon Fair).
OS Map 124. GR 666 405.

Dedicated to the Virgin Mother despite the old village church being named after St Twrog, brother to St Trillo, a fervent disciple of St Beuno and who died in 610AD. It is said to be an exception to most of the other Welsh wells and springs dedicated to St Mary in that it runs towards the west instead of south. Wells with their outlets to the south were also believed to possess the most powerful healing properties. This well supplied the village of Maentwrog (Welsh for Twrog's Stone which is propped up close to the church door), in the Vale of Ffestiniog on the A496, with clean domestic water for many years.

Appearing to grow almost organically out of the steep hillside, the chamber is a 1.5m cube constructed from large slabs of the local dark-grey slate and covered over with another of the same. An outlet near the top ensures a good head of water is contained within and an old-fashioned tap near the bottom allows water to be drawn when the water table becomes somewhat depleted.

There is a bit of a climb to see this one but at least it is fairly close to the road. If you stand under the clock set in the churchyard gate and face the War Memorial opposite, turn to the right and walk about 20m. A steep flight of wide slate steps will be on your left. Go up these to a name-plate stating you are facing Box Tree House then turn right to follow a path through a small grassy area to a junction with a wider track.

Turn right again and a few metres will bring you to a steep public footpath on the left leading up into the trees above. The well is on the right only a few metres up.

* St Mary's Well
(Ffynnon Fair).
OS Map 123. GR 226 313.   *Anglesey*

Starting from Pwllheli, go west along the A499, take the B4413 right at Llanbedrog and follow this road through Mynytho and Botwnnog to Sarn Meyllteyrn. Keep on the same road through the village and turn into the first left about 2km further into Bryncroes. By the village green you will see a bridge over a little brook and St Mary's well is just over the bridge on the right.

On a mound to one side is Bethel Chapel, built on the same site as the original place of worship founded when the spring, as it was then, was consecrated.

The well itself is open-topped and about 4m square with a well chamber not quite 2m square in the middle. It is walled to a height of a metre or so with a paved walkway round the chamber reached by a couple of steps. The water at present is not very deep and makes its exit along by the bridge wall to the brook a few metres away. It is a neat little well and was used by the villagers in fairly recent times. Little is known of any alleged healing properties.

St Mary's Well
(Ffynnon Fair).
OS Map 148. GR 256 683.

Anyone who visits this well will agree that the serene atmosphere of its setting and present condition would make it a perfect candidate for refurbishment. It is an ancient-seeming well in the graveyard of the old church of Pilleth overlooking the upper valley of the River Lugg.

This squat, plain, yet very photogenic church dedicated to St Mary stands on the hillside a couple of kilometres west of the village of Whitton on the B4356. The town of Presteigne is about 8km further east of the village. It isn't hard to miss seeing it as you approach - but the turning to it is. You must go past the entrance to Pilleth Court and Farm (on the right) and a couple of hundred metres further on there will be a sharp turn to the right up a grassy lane, at present indicated by a weathered and rather indistinct finger-post. This will lead you a couple of hundred metres to a small turning area in front of the church.

Go into the churchyard up a flight of interesting stone steps and then to the other side of the building. Both building and steps are constructed out of smaller bits of masonry than usual in Wales and give an impression of being tightly-packed. The well is in the shadow of the square bell tower, close to the church wall. At present it more strongly resembles an open grave than a "sacred" well. Rectangular in shape and quite large, a flight of five worn steps leads down to the water nearly 2m below ground level.

The shallow pool is a bit over a metre square and fed from the side furthest away from the steps where the wall is composed of raw bed-rock. Both side are masonry and evidently close to a state of collapse, necessitating the use of heavy timbers to act as a buttress. A wooden safety handrail marks the limit of sensible approach from the sides.

A couple of ancient mounds close by are probably of a similar age as the well. Because of its location and surroundings it is suspected that it has always been of the "sacred" variety without pagan associations. Good for eyes, it has been claimed; in what way is not clear.

St Mary's Well
(Ffynnon Fair).
OS Map 125. GR 104 065.

One of the "Great Little Trains of Wales", as fondly called by the late, and greatly missed Wynford Vaughan Thomas in his popular TV series, starts (or ends, depending on which way you are going) at Llanfair Caereinion in the Banwy valley. In 1990 the Prince of Wales, in his capacity of Chairman of the Prince of Wales Committee, gave Royal Approval to a restoration of the noted well here.

It occupies a small ledge cut into a high bank overlooking the rushing rocky river, and a grand job they made of it too. L-shaped and lined with dressed masonry it is about 5m long and 2m across the widest section. A set of steps descend the long section of the "L" to the water which appears to be a metre or so deep.

A metal grid, hinged to allow access to the full depth when required, ensures it is not possible to drown if you fall in. Trees almost surround the well and a long stone seat at the far end gives relative ease to those who wish to stay and meditate a while. A riverside walk is through a gate near the seat.

No pagan connection can be ascertained but there is certainly a strong religious one. The church is dedicated to St Mary and there has been a proper stone building on the site since at least the 12th century, and probably a couple of less enduring ones before that. Parts of this known early one still survive incorporated into the present structure.

Llanfair Caereinion is situated on the A458 west of Welshpool and is also approached by the B4389 from Newtown to the south.

The well is in the corner of the churchyard on the High Street. Go through the gate to the church door and turn left. A set of thirty steps will lead you down to a platform above the river. The spring water here has been used for baptisms both in the church and sometimes the pool is opened for collective total immersion ceremonies. It was reputed to be efficacious in the cure of skin complaints and rheumatism.

Perhaps more importantly in ancient times, prayers and devotions, accompanied by a donation to Church funds, would protect the applicant against witchcraft and curses; a practice which some who cannot cope with today's social attitudes, taxes and over-regulation would be advised to revive.

It worked once, they say. Why shouldn't it do so again?

St Mary's Well
(Ffynnon Fair).
OS Map 145. GR 317 540.

Also known as Ffynnon-y-Groes (Spring of the Cross) from the time when St Carantoc made the sign of the Cross when he drank from the spring, liked what he saw of the area and promptly claimed the patch for himself. Close to the spring he founded his own timber church in the 6th century; the present one dates from 1885.

It happened to be on one of the main routes for pilgrims travelling along the edge of Cardigan Bay to and from St Davids - a fact which would not have escaped the notice of St Carantoc. At this point on the Cardiganshire cliffs there is a distinct shortage of water courses for several kilometres on either side so the spring became an important stopping place. St Carantoc's gesture of obeisance caught the imagination of the pilgrims; it became a habit at the well and before long all visitors were obliged to make the sign of the Cross before drinking. It didn't take much more to raise the status of the well to that of a "healing" well for divers ailments.

A small community known as Llangranog grew up and became a fishing and boat-building harbour. This part of Cardigan Bay is not noted for its wide expanses of sandy golden strand, rock and cliffs predominate, but there is a small beach here. Consequently, this potentially pretty little village crammed into a narrow cleft eroded by the diminutive River Hawen has become very popular with tourists in the area.

A helpful pamphlet has been produced which gives the visitor useful information about places of interest in the vicinity. Fynnon Fair is marked on it - but just try to see where it is!

Proper directions are thus: if you leave the A487 at Pentregat and follow the B4321 down into the village (about 6km) you will see the church sitting in a rather untidy churchyard on the right. At the beginning of the churchyard is a house called Pont Fair, opposite which is an old bridge over the brook. A garage built on stilts over the brook is a good landmark. Immediately after crossing the bridge and before an opening into the field on the left force your head through the thicket and, if you are very lucky, you may just about be able to see where the spring rises among a scatter of almost buried masonry only a matter of 2m away.

And that is all that's left of Ffynnon Fair - the original reason for the existence of the village and revered by many devout folk through the ages. A "sacred" well is certainly a legitimate candidate for entry in a tourist pamphlet but not when it has been subjected to such disgraceful neglect as this. If it cannot be restored for visitors to enjoy then the decent thing would be to remove it from all tourist literature entirely and allow it to be quietly forgotten in dignity.

* St Mary's Well
(Ffynnon Fair).
OS Map 116. GR 029 711.

Certainly the most photogenic of the few remaining Welsh wells dedicated to St Mary and arguably one of the more interesting ones. A glance at the Ordnance Survey map would suggest that it is situated to the south of the River Elwy outside the small cathedral town of St Asaph, but this is incorrect.

From the mini-roundabout in St Asaph just off the A55, take the B5381 in a southerly direction along the Elwy valley. After about 2.5km, turn into the first proper right-hand road you come to just before the river bridge (and a hair-raising double bend) and follow the lane for half a kilometre to where the lane starts to climb through trees. Don't go up the hill but walk along the signposted public footpath for about 300m down to a gate across the track just past a couple of houses.

It is at the end of the first meadow beyond this gate, where a rill passes over the track (once known as the Cat's Path, for some obscure reason) by a small red-roofed farm building. The old chapel (built around 1550, though traces of older masonry from the early 1400s can be seen at the base of the walls) can be seen on the right at the base of a wooded slope 70m or so away. Built from an attractive shade of stone, the remaining walls are surrounded by railing with an entrance gate on the left side. The well can be seen beyond this gate.

It consists of two distinct chambers. The larger one has five angular recesses on three of its sides, believed at one time to represent the five porches of the Pool of Bethesda. The salient outer points are made of flat stones roughly chiselled to the shape of a cross which used to act as supports for fluted arches with a decorated canopy - a smaller version of the inner chamber at St Winifred's Well. The same architect seems to have been commissioned for both jobs and it would be no surprise to discover that the cash needed for the job came in the form of a hand-out from that much wealthier holy water business to the east.

With a depth of about a metre, the water surface is nearly half a metre below ground level and the whole thing is approximately 3m across in any direction.. At the bottom of this attractive and limpid pool is a layer of a rather peculiar sediment - not quite sand nor mud - creamy in colour and in places scattered on the strands of a dark water weed sprouting here and there. It is suspected that this is a precipitation from the water itself rather than sediment being pushed up by the spring. Bursts of clear bubbles often rise from the bottom at irregular intervals, sometimes in quite large quantities.

To one side is a much smaller chamber from which water was probably drawn for baptisms and the like. The water exits from here now but the original overflow from the large chamber contains two dressed and strangely curved stones, the significance of which is obscure. Entering a small gully, the rill then curves for a few metres before straightening out to flow along the western chapel wall inside the chapel; a very unusual feature. In fact, the church used to be of the cruciform variety; the well under its canopy also being within one arm of the walls.

One authority states that "clandestine marriages" were held here in the present chapel's early days. This could be a reference to a local lady of sinister repute who lived for a while in a large, fine house (Dol Belidr - now approaching a

St Mary's Well, St Aspath

ruinous condition) just over the river who was married there more than once. She got through husbands at an alarming rate. No sooner had she married one but she was on the lookout for a successor. The long procession of unsuspecting husbands were rendered redundant by a series of ingenious terminations. It is alleged that one was painfully transformed into the deceased state by pouring molten lead into one of his ears as he slept; but the full saga is far too gruesome to go into here. In such a peaceful and pleasant setting as this little chapel with its interesting well it is hard to give the story any real credence - but it really did happen, so they say.

A small dwelling house which once stood a bit to the southwest of the church served as home to a succession of priests and well-guardians.

St Mary Magdalene's Well
(Ffynnon Fair Fagdalen).
OS Map 116. GR 954 490.

A poor thing but still there. From the A5 at Cerrigydrudion take the B4501 signed for Llyn Brenig and look out for the village school on the right. Directly opposite there is a footpath gate to enter the field and a stone wall inside on the left. Follow the wall downhill for about 50m to where it turns to the left under a sycamore tree and the remains of the well are inside the field on the corner of the wall under the tree.

Not much is left; only a few scattered stones surround a dry hollow. The tree roots seem to have diverted the water but there is a seepage only a few metres away. The old sill is still there, however; a large thin stone on edge about a metre long lying embedded across the downhill side. There is a V-shaped notch in the centre from which the water used to exit the chamber.

Cerrigydrudion means "Crag of the Warriors" in English so the immediate area must have been of some importance in military terms. Where the crag has gone is anybody's guess though it is probable that the mound on which the church now stands could have merited the name. Druids had sacred wells here too, so it is somewhat surprising that of the three which have been recorded in the village only two remain and both of them are badly treated even though the village church is dedicated to St Mary Magdalene. The original stone well is said to have had steps down to the water and two standing stones alongside as one would have expected at an important Druidic water-hole.

This well should not take much to restore. A small pond liner, willing juvenile helpers from the school only 50m away and a rearrangement of the stones is all that is required. Hint, hint.

The other remaining well is also dry except after rain. It is said to have been called Ffynnon Brawd (Brother's Spring), possibly after a resident monk or friar who wished to remain anonymous. It remains unnoticed even though the main A5 carrying thousands of vehicles a day passes only 10m away.

Next to the Saracen's Head hotel on the A5 is Jerusalem chapel. Directly opposite, on the other side of the road from the chapel is a small field within which can be seen a small huddle of dry-stone walling close to the ground. Ffynnon Brawd: nearly forgotten - until now. It was said to be good for warts - removing them, that is.

St Michael's Well
(Ffynnon Fihangel).
OS Map 124 GR 706 437.

Although within only a very few metres of the main A470 trunk road between Llan Ffestiniog and Blaenau Ffestiniog this well, highly respected up to the beginning of the 20th century, cannot be seen from there. Access was once available from the road but now a visitor would have to go into the grounds of an adjoining farmhouse called Ffynnon Farm in order to view it across Nant Manod brook.

The spring rises under the floor within the crumbling ruin of an old cottage called Ffynnondwr (Spring Water) which was occupied up until about 1890. The water exits from a pipe into the adjacent brook and was once in great demand for the cure of paralysis, fits, fractured limbs and, as always, rheumatism. A stone bridge, now unfortunately swept away by the brook during a flood, connected the cottage with the opposite bank until only a few years ago. Unless you take a pair of Wellington boots the cottage is effectively out of reach for a close examination.

To find it go north along the A470 from Llan Ffestiniog towards Blaenau Ffestiniog. About 1.5km after leaving the last houses in Llan Ffestiniog look out for a sweeping double bend rising up a slope with a farm gate on the right at the bottom leading to Ffynnon Uchaf (the name is on the gate). On the left there is a large layby to put the car. Ffynnon Fihangel is almost directly opposite the gate below road level and cannot be seen due to a dense covering of Japanese knotweed and other tangled undergrowth.

The present owner of the farmhouse seen just beyond the well, Mrs Hughes, will be pleased to grant permission to view. A gate signposted Ffynnon Farm gives access.

Strenuous efforts are being made at the time of writing to try and arrange for the restoration of this worthy site but it is rather a big job by well-restoration standards. The problem is, as always, a lack of sufficient ready cash. If there are any well-philanthropists out there, please make yourselves known.

St Moling's Well
(Ffynnon Myllin).
OS Map 125. GR 139 196.

The market town of Llanfyllin straddles the A490 about 20km north-west of Welshpool. Despite the recent introduction of that phony Lego-land "antique street furniture" it still remains an attractive place to visit. At the centre, in the town square, stands the Cain Valley Hotel.

Opposite the hotel is Market Street. Go up here to the end (about 100m) and turn right. Keep turning right and you will enter a cul-de-sac leading up a hill. The top section is rather steep but where the tarmac ends, about 300m from the town square, St Moling's well will be on your left.

It is a very pretty and grassy landscaped area, complete with little artificial waterfall fed from the spring and overlooking the town. Seats are placed in strategic positions making it a pleasant spot to enjoy the view and watch the day go by. Under a large sycamore tree growing from the bank is the well chamber.

Entered through a low arch not much more than a metre high, the interior penetrates the bank for nearly 2m with a platform on the left. The sides are lined with rough stone blocks and the trickle of spring water tumbles from a projecting stone into a shallow pool which takes up the rest of the floor area. In 1987, Llanfyllin Town Council's restoration of the site won the prestigious Prince of Wales award - and deservedly so.

Moling Luachair was a very highly respected Irish saint. He is said to have been the first to use baptism in Britain and used this well for the purpose during the 6th century - according to a plaque at the site. Its medical properties are alleged to be multiple and this is one of the few "rag wells" (where the sick left parts of their clothing hanging as offerings from the surrounding bushes) still existing.

Llanfyllin is in the old county of Montgomeryshire where a Trinity Sunday tradition was to visit the local holy well, tip in a lot of sugar provided by females of the parish, drink as much as you wanted and then get involved with open air games and competitions. This was the case at Moling's well. The recipients of this annual boon, the males (who also participated the most energetically in the games), were then expected to return the favour by treating their benefactors to a beer and cake bonanza at the local boozer. This sounds like a charming custom which should be revived as soon as possible.

The well is sometimes called Ffynnon Coed y Llan (Parish Woods Spring) and is said to have been able to foretell the future but the correct ritual needed for this seems to have been forgotten over the years.

The water is certainly very refreshing after the slog up that short but merciless hill and a good feed at the Cain Valley Hotel should satisfyingly complete your visit to Llanfyllin.

Monk's Well
(Ffynnon y Mynach).
OS Map 148. GR 224 434.

The Romans had to have a supply of fresh water close at hand wherever they established their garrisons, just like anybody else. This spring is nice and handy for one of their larger forts built close to the River Wye at Hay-on-Wye and was taken over by the monks who founded a monastery there when the Romans picked up their marbles and went home.

From the town of Hay, go over the river bridge on the B4351 and take the first right after half a kilometre. Another half kilometre or so along a narrow lane will bring you to the entrance of Ti'r Mynach (Monk's House) farm on the left.

The well is hard to spot straight away but you will notice a small flow of water under the track by the entrance gate. Look left to where this originates and a rectangular structure will be made out within the bushes standing in a fairly wide area of water seepage. This is the well that sustained hundreds of homesick Roman shock-troops and all the monks who came after to try an invasion of religion after tough-guy tactics had paved the way. Later it was used by the locals for assisting in the cure of eye problems and the ubiquitous rheumatism.

There is little else to say regarding the sad state of this one.

Newcastle Well
OS Map 161. GR 443 172.

The village of Newcastle is located on the B4347 about 11km north-west of Monmouth town. Turn left down a narrow country lane alongside a public house and go down to the first field gate on the left (about 200m). Look out over the field and the once-famous Newcastle well will be seen in a hollow half way across the field.

On the brow of the hill above stands a mound which is all that remains of an ancient timber fortress said to be haunted by evil folk desirous of expunging the sins they committed when alive. The "little people" (fairies) were said to have taken the well under their protection and endowed it with many powers of healing. Sufferers came from afar to test the validity of this assertion and many miraculous cures have been attributed to its waters. The history of this site's continued use goes way back into pagan times.

It is therefore most disappointing to see the sorry state it is in today. The hollow in the area of the water outlet has been used as a tip for small heaps of building rubble - a most unpleasant sight for what is, to many, a part of our heritage; such an important site now befouled and unattractive. If the present increasing awareness of sites of historical interest continues to grow, this is a place which could really do with a face-lift to help preserve one of those things which meant so much to our ancestors.

* Nine Wells
(Naw Ffynhonnau).
OS Map 157. GR 786 248.

The region of Nine Wells in Pembrokeshire was not a healthy place to be if you happened to be a maiden under twelve years of age during pagan times.

Central to the area stood a cromlech with a sinister reputation; a burial chamber from an early time. Here, every so often and according to the whim of the local witch-doctor, a dozen maidens under the age of puberty were sacrificed by ordeal of fire. The cromlech and altar stone where the maidens were burnt have been removed for some time now, probably supporting a farm gate or acting as a lintel somewhere today, their bloodthirsty past unsuspected by the present owners.

Most of the nine wells once here have also disappeared, only one remaining within easy view. It is close to the side of the A487 in the village just past Solva on the way to St Davids. At the bottom of a dip in the road turn left on to a track leading to a camp site and the well can just about be made out at the edge of a thicket on the right no more than 10m away across a small grassy area on the junction.

It is in the shape of an arch, overgrown and built of stone, about 2m high and 1.5m wide. At the base of the square opening is a sill-slab worn with a deep hollow by much use. Inside is a shallow pool of clear water about half a metre square, evidently much lower in level than it used to be. This is probably one of the wells where mass was celebrated during the Age of Saints. Water was taken from this well to St Davids cathedral and used for washing down the shrine of the patron saint of Wales.

The nine wells were in a handy place for the multitude of pilgrims on their way to the shrine as they were the last watering place on the route. Rosaries were dipped in the "sacred" waters and it became a favoured stopping point for sick pilgrims who bathed there (some of the wells must have been a lot bigger than the one still on view) before going on to the cathedral to be blessed by the resident priest. Many of these sufferers would also be enjoined to carry on to St Non's well a short distance away as part of their treatment.

There is no doubt this has been a very important site for many purposes over the ages. A visit here can be further enjoyed by taking the footpath south through a pretty National Trust valley to the little cove of Porth-y-Rhaw less than a kilometre away.

St Noe's Well
OS Map 161. GR 460 210.

Located on the B4521 about halfway between Abergavenny and Ross-on-Wye, Skenfrith is an important venue for those with an interest in antiquities, due mostly to the squat old castle guarding this narrow section of the Monnow valley and a working water mill.

Although Noe's well is not, strictly speaking, in Wales, it is within a few metres of the present-day border and only a short way from the village where St Noe set out her religious stall. Any such fine distinction is academic really because no border existed in Noe's time except that enforced by the strong arms and gnashing teeth of the Cymric tribes against invaders. She occasioned a chapel to be built there together with a bridge enabling her to gain access to the well even during times of flood.

Directions to the well are - from Skenfrith castle, travel west along the B4521 past the pub, over the river bridge and take the first left up a narrow lane just before the Priory Hotel. After about 1.5km, the woods on your right will end and the well is tucked tightly in the corner of a field by the edge of the trees. It is a bit difficult to see through the hedge but take the end of the trees as a guide and you can't miss it.

It still falls just within the technical definition of a well because the main water flow comes from between two smallish square-cut stones. A peculiarity is the regular eruptions of bubbles, sometimes many in number and sometimes large enough to splash drops of water into the air. The rest of the pool is a muddy circle about 8m in diameter. There are several other water outlets scattered in front of the main one where small "geysers" constantly welling from beneath have constructed little volcano-shaped mounds of clean sediment differing in colour from the surrounding mud.

In the early part of the 19th century local children were kept in order by a tale that the witch of the well would carry them away if they misbehaved. This "witch" - either a hermitess with a bad press or possibly the "priestess" of the well who took her duties too seriously - was said to live in the woods nearby and would watch until a pilgrim's attention was diverted before attacking the unsuspecting visitor with a stick.

From this tale it may be assumed this was a "healing" as well as a "sacred" well, though no details of its virtues have been located as yet.

* St Non's Well

(Ffynnon Non).
Festival Day 3rd March.
OS Map 157. GR 751 243.

Like her illustrious son David, patron saint of Wales, St Non's life has as many differing versions as there are authorities to speculate upon them. It has even been suggested that Non was David's father but if that were so then the rest of this entry is nonsense. Even her name is asserted by some to be "Nun" - a reference to her calling rather than her given name. She was also known as Nonna, and sometimes Nonni, allegedly a grand-daughter of the excessively virile Brychan Brycheiniog. David's father is generally acknowledged to be called Sandde, a prince and one of the grandsons of Cunedda Wledig. Some say he was Non's husband but others darkly assert she was brutally ravished by the prince against her will.

Even the place she gave birth to David has been a matter of dispute but in such differences of opinion lies the interest of history. The most often quoted version states that David came into this world some time around 500AD (others say 520AD) under the most inauspicious of omens. A savage thunderstorm raged at the time Non suddenly came into labour on the cliff-top above the Pembrokeshire bay which now bears her name. David's first view of the world was one of tempest, fury and elemental ruin, but both mother and son survived the ordeal.

The spot he was born is said to be the site of an ancient ruined chapel, some of which still stands there on the windswept cliffs, and at the exact moment of his birth a holy spring erupted from the ground close by.

The chapel and well are signposted from the cathedral in St Davids; a journey of about a kilometre. A small car park is at the end of the lane near a building called "St Non's Retreat" which has its own chapel. The ancient monuments are within 100m from the car park and can be easily seen from there.

The well is the closest at the far end of a little area of consecrated ground beyond a gate at the bottom of a rather steep footpath. In July 1951 it was re-dedicated with due reverence after an extensive restoration. At the same time an official pilgrimage was arranged in which devout representatives from many parts of the world took part. It is an attractive location with two of the characteristic Pembroke shrine-domes facing each other across an open space. That nearest the gate houses a white statue of the saint, beautifully presented, while the other contains the ancient well.

The arch over the well is no more than 1.5m in any dimension yet the water chamber seems surprisingly large by comparison. It is about a metre deep and evidently still much used as evident by the many coins which have been offered together with the usual dispensations of small white pebbles, fragments of shell and little white flowers. Every wish is said to be granted eventually as long as an offering is made and strict silence maintained until the supplicant returns home.

The dome is relatively new but some of the lower masonry in front of the well has been worn smooth by the passage of time and use. A kneeling stone lies directly in front of the chamber and just behind this is a small and shallow rectangular pool

St Non's Well, St Davids

permitting easier access to the water for the infirm. At one time stone seats surrounded the well where patients waited for a cure. Said to deal successfully with many diseases, the water exhibits no particular mineral properties of any abundance though a south Wales chemist ensured his pension by selling the real stuff (so he said) from his shop at the beginning of the 20th century. His advertising blurb assured prospective customers that it would cure headaches and rheumatism - a natural result of being properly consecrated.

No salt can be tasted - even though the well is alleged to ebb and flow with the tide. But this would be miraculous indeed if it happened because the sea level cannot be much less than 40m below the level of the well. Visitors were naturally expected to make a cash payment to the custodian of the well who lived in a cottage at the top of the field with a good view of any "poachers" trying to get cured for free. There was great competition for the job because St Non's well was considered to be one of the most lucrative wells in Wales.

The miraculous cures obtained there were said to work best on St David's day, March 1st. The last recorded healings were in 1860 when both a man and a boy hobbled painfully there on a pilgrimage, did all the right things and paid out their cash, then walked back home leaving their crutches by the well. One cannot but suspect that the well was by then becoming less popular and the whole thing could have been a put-up job to drum up some extra business; but who can be certain of this?

Just the other side of the farther gate is the old chapel which has a curious stone slab propped up in one corner with a Celtic cross inscribed thereupon. Evidence of many repairs and rebuilding over the long ages can be observed in the many differing stone sizes and styles of construction even in the few bits of wall that are left. Several standing stones are in the near vicinity though the authenticity of these is somewhat suspect in spite of the area being known as highly religiously important during pagan times.

After founding several Welsh nunneries Non went to Cornwall, founded a few more then left for Brittany where she died in the late 6th century.

St Non's Well
(Ffynnon Non).
OS Map 159. GR 540 083.

From Crosshands roundabout on the A48 take the A476 south towards Llanelli for about 6km to Llanon village. Turn left at the Greyhound public house into Fountain Road (Heol Ffynnon), down a short, steep hill for 50m and the site of St Non's well is on the right.

It is said that St Non, Mother of David, patron saint of Wales, used this well and founded a church eventually superseded by the nearby square-towered church dedicated to her. Evidently it must have been a natural spring at that time and much later provided the fledgling village with their water supply. In 1889, the friends of a Mr Rhys Goring Thomas erected the present shrine-like fountain to fulfil his last wish that the village would always have a plentiful supply of water. Words to this effect can be seen on the fountain which did its job faithfully for many years. A pipe protruding from the centre of the small but admirable structure tipped water into a small rectangular trough.

No other verifiable virtues for this well have so far been traced.

St Padarn's Well
(Ffynnon Badarn).
Festival Day Apr 15th.
OS Map 135. GR594 813.

Now dried up since it helped to provide water for the village of Llanbadarn Fawr, a suburb of the university town of Aberystwyth. Extensive building on the hillside above must be responsible for this.

It is directly on the roadside on the left of the A44 between Aberystwyth and Llanbadarn Fawr about half a kilometre from the church of St Padarn. Set into the retaining wall is a small arch within which is an outlet pipe and a trough built by the local Sanitary Authority in 188-something.

Used in olden days for its medical qualities, St Padarn's spring gave good service over the generations until destroyed by "civilisation". The saint himself was French and came over in the 5th century with a gaggle of other missionaries to save the Welsh from total depravity. First an abbot, then a bishop, he founded the old monastery at Llanbadarn Fawr which became a major centre of religious learning and studies. Many are the churches dedicated to him and the big lake at Llanberis is also in his name.

St Padarn died in 550AD and was buried (in that order) with full honours on the island of deceased saints - Bardsey (Ynys Enlli).

(Lord) Penrhyn's Well
(Ffynnon Penrhyn).
OS Map 116 GR 842 488.

Ysbyty Ifan is best known for the ancient hospice (some say hospital, but the correct designation is Hospitium Sancti

Ioannis) founded by the Knights of the Hospital of St John of Jerusalem to provide succour and accommodation for the "Pilgrims of Wales". Much later, historically speaking, it became the centre of activity by a bunch of professional bandits who terrorised the neighbourhood for generations until ousted by a force led by Meredydd ap Ifan, a local tough guy. The few survivors fled to Dinas Mawddwy in mid-Wales where they started up the family business all over again. It is probable all used this little spring for a fresh water supply.

Known locally as Pistyll-y-Llan (Parish fountain), the name was changed in 1866 when Lord Penrhyn (slate master of Penrhyn Castle, Bangor, fame), who also owned the huge grouse moors of the Migneint above the village, made provision for a proper hygienic spout his serfs could use. This was long before health-consciousness began climbing to the peak of hysterical paranoia it enjoys today but Ysbyty Ifan was a "hospital" village, and had a reputation to keep up. Dead serfs aren't much good at farming or mining slate, after all, and one cannot help but wonder how the locals managed to put enough pressure on the mighty lord. Serfs usually come cheaper than wells.

It is in the shape of an arched recess by the roadside in the bank of a field. Less than 2m high or wide it has a nameplate and a pipe which delivers a small but constant supply of cold, very sweet water. Some folk still use it for their own purposes.

The great musician and Welsh hymn writer T. Osborne-Roberts, husband of the noted soprano Leila Magane (real name Bessy Jones), wrote a song about this spring in the early 1900s which his wife performed at some of their concerts.

Unless you know exactly where Ysbyty Ifan is, the best place to start from would be Betws-y-Coed. Go east along the A5 in the direction of Llangollen for about 8km and branch left on the B4407 which is signposted for Ysbyty Ifan. A bit over 3km will bring you to the cross-roads at the entrance of the village and Ffynnon Penrhyn will be seen on the right just after the cross-roads.

* St Peris's Well
(Ffynnon Beris).
OS Map115. GR 609 583.

Just to the east of the Vaynol Arms in Nant Peris (Old Llanberis) is a neat car park among the trees. It is on the A4086 at the bottom of Llanberis Pass. From the car park, turn right at the entrance and walk just over a hundred metres to the first gate on the left. It is marked "Tan-y-Fedwen" and gives access to a public footpath. Another hundred metres or so along a rough track will bring you to a pretty little cottage seeming to grow out of the surrounding rocks. Just past this is the well on the left, once called Ffynnon-y-Sant (Saint's Well) by some. It is not a spring here; the little brook which feeds it coming from a bit further up where seepage issues from a wide area of spongy marsh.

St Peris was a crony of St Padarn and the two lakes in this spectacular glaciated valley are named after each of them. His well was famous in its day and sometimes contained fish (some say trout - others eels). This is hardly surprising because trout often find their way up here from Llyn Peris during the spawning season and eels manage to get almost anywhere where there is a bit of water.

The fish were said to be sacred, their absence when visiting boding no good for the purpose for which the pilgrim came there. Obviously a matter of chance as in all wells where fish are supposed to be included in the ritual. Local poachers were discouraged by the application of gross physical ill-treatment and/or severe pain.

175

A slightly different version of the story of the fish (known as Ty'nyffynnon fishes) is that they were two trout which were put in the well at the same time and fed by the guardian of the well. When one of them died (their average lifetime was said to be about fifty years) no other was put in until the other one also died. They were always stocked in pairs. The last of these trout is alleged to have died near the beginning of the 20th century - it was blind due to old age and over 43cms in length.

The well is a rude structure at a change in the course of the rill which comes in at one end under the wall and exits through a side wall. It is quite deep and big enough for total immersion which is what the rituals for curing most diseases required. A cash payment would be given to the "priestess" and another, larger donation put into the alms chest in the cruciform parish church a short distance away.

Children were the main supplicants here, coming in hope to get rid of the scourge of rickets but grown people also used the place to assist in the cure of rheumatism, warts, tumours and TB. Festivals were celebrated by the well, drunken ones for the most part - except on Holy days, of course.

* St Peter's Well
(Ffynnon Bedr).
OS Map 170. GR 795 865.

At Junction 38 on the M4 take the eastbound A48 and then the first turning left about 100m from the motorway roundabout. Keep left along this tarmac lane and take the second turning left. A short hill will bring you to a rutted track leading off to the left. It is not recommended that a car be taken any further but the spring is only a short walk along this track.

About 200m along the track a small well-pit will be seen on the right hand side under the trees. This is not St Peter's well; you will have to walk about the same distance further, around a bend, and when the track straightens look out for a spring rather than a "well" a few metres off the track on the left (St Peter's well is more of a spring than anything else). The spring itself is uncared for, neglected, and some of the filthier locals have deposited trash in the immediate area; a common pastime in this section of Wales.

It is in woodland on the south-west flank of Graig Fawr mountain to the west of Margam Abbey. These pleasant woods are full of bluebells in the springtime which goes a long way to improving the otherwise unprepossessing foreground close to the roar of traffic on the M4 motorway and the noise and fumes from the huge steelworks at Port Talbot.

Little is known of the history of this well other than the fact it is dedicated to St Peter - whether by the man himself or one of his "groupies" who wished to extend Peter's influence. Probably the latter. Healing? Maybe, but not known for sure. Any other customs? Again, don't know, but there is no reason to suppose the locals were any different in their beliefs to elsewhere. What is known is that the immediate area was very important to the Celts who left standing stones, circles and hill forts all over the place. Later, when organised religion initiated a hostile take-over, the impressive Abbey (open to the public) was built close by and the place suddenly became overrun with monks.

The "well" itself is a simple arrangement. The water reaches the open air through a small portico constructed of a couple of flat stones topped with another and runs in a shallow furrow through the trees. There is no sign of water on the other side of the track. This is a well that badly needs adopting and looking after for future generations.
Any takers?

* St Peter's Well
(Ffynnon Bedr).
OS Map 146. GR 571 477.

The regional market town of Lampeter (Llanbedr) is justly proud of the widely respected theological college at its centre. Religious students attend from all over the world to learn from its teachings. Few, if any, visit the sacred well of St Peter languishing in unforgivable decay within easy walking distance of the campus.

From the town centre take the A475 to the southern edge of town. Just after the last house on the right there is a small cemetery and a few metres beyond this is a gate on the left allowing access to a track running between two neat lines of tall trees. A couple of hundred metres down the track is another gate.

Standing at this second gate, look across to the left at about 10 o'clock and you will see some ruins in a small grove of trees. This is all that is left of the building called Peterwell, once the seat of local authority. In the same line of sight, out in the field and about 30m beyond the ruins lies the well of St Peter. In total, it is about 250m level walk from the road.

The well is now little more than a hollow in the ground, choked with grass and surrounded by the remains of a masonry wall. A shallow, muddy pool lies beneath. It is about 4m across and the bottom is about a metre below ground level. No stories of medicinal virtue have been verified.

* St Peter's Well
(Ffynnon Bedr).
OS Map 115. GR approx 76/69.

Although the farm with the same name is marked on the Ordnance Survey map, this once famous well is no longer open to casual visitors at the time of writing. It is about half a kilometre south of the church at Llanbedr-y-cennin in the lower Conway valley. Still overshadowed by the old yew always associated with this well, it was once covered by building for privacy. Cures for children are said to have been many, the procedure being total immersion then an overnight stop in a nearby well chapel.

Rocky Well
(Ffynnon y Garreg).
OS Map 161. GR 303 138.

On entering the town of Abergavenny along the A40 from the south you will spy the bus terminus and car park on the right. Starting from here, turn left at the exit on to the main road, cross the bridge over the little River Gafenni and almost immediately turn left again into Holywell Road. A matter of 100m or so along this road will bring you to the well on the right hand side. Easy access for those in a wheelchair.

It is in the form of two troughs fed by a pipe leading from a collecting chamber and pleasantly planted around with flowers tended by a person living close by. It is sited at the bottom of the front garden of a house called "Prior's Well" built in 1947. The meadow where the house now stands was once called "Hole in the wall meadow" at the time of the Reformation and the road - only a narrow lane at that time - "Hole in the wall Lane". The similarity between "Hole in the wall" and "Holywell" is obvious and one cannot help but wonder which came first and is therefore the original designation.

In 1901, a local man called Mr Foster built a horse trough to catch and retain the flow from the spring. At that time it trickled out of a low rock outcrop (now covered) and this feature gave this site yet another name - Ffynnon-y-Garreg. Long before the Reformation, monks from the old priory a couple of hundred metres away across the River Gafenni by the present church dedicated to St Mary used to collect water from here for drinking purposes. This gave rise to a further name - Ffynnon Fair (St Mary's well).

Whatever name you choose to call it, this little spring has been important for a long time - even up to today. It never dries up or freezes. When the present occupier of "Prior's Well" moved in during 1961 old people from the town regularly used to collect water for medicinal purposes. Particularly good for eyes, by all accounts. Even after this time, a farm lad on his way to market with cattle from about 15km away always used to stop here to give the herd a final drink before being sold. It helped to put a bit of weight on them too, of course. Appropriately enough, the A40 at this point used to be one of the major drovers' roads from Wales and a dependable supply of water close to a grassy watermeadow would have been a favourite stopping place - particularly with the notorious ale taverns and harlots of old Abergavenny being only a short staggering distance away.

A plaque over the well says "This historic Holy Well was restored by the Abergavenny Civic Society in 1988".

Roman Baths, Margam
OS Map 170. GR 803 869.

At Junction 38 on the M4 take the eastbound A48 and then the first turning left about 100m from the motorway roundabout. Keep left along this paved lane and take the second turning left. Go past a gate-house and a small lake on the right (said to be arranged to flood an underground escape tunnel from the castle in the event of hostile pursuit), up a steep hill and take the first turning right on this hill. The lane descends through woodland and after about 100m or so, near the bottom of the slope, you will see a wooden-fenced enclosure on the right and a small masonry structure, the roof of which is on the same level as the lane.

An interesting arrangement, this. A small arched entrance allows access to the interior which is also arched. It is about 8m long; the far end consisting of a deep sunken "bath" to which one can descend by means of steps. From the far wall pours a spout of water which has never been known to run dry even in the most drought-ridden of summers. There is no evidence of a water-course uphill of the spot.

Looking at the arrangement, one can be in no doubt that this must have been intended to give total immersion of the body, yet there is some dispute over the origin - could it actually be a Roman Baths or did Monks from Margam Abbey construct it? Even medieval monks probably felt the need of a good scrub-down at times. Or could it be a sacred well dedicated to St Mary (Fair), as some assert, and associated with an ancient chapel called Capel Mair not far away? To reach this chapel, walk up the hill from the well back to the main lane and a path will be seen on the opposite side a few metres down. A short and not very steep walk will bring you to the chapel ruins where Mass is still celebrated every midsummer, according to a local resident.

The most likely name for this well, however, is Ffynnon Gyffyr, and was apparently listed as such in the Archaeologia Cambrensis during 1914.

It is said that baptisms were once carried out in the little well building (there is enough room inside) or water may have been carried up to the chapel from the well for the same purpose - or both. At present the well could do with some refurbishing but it is definitely interesting enough for a visit at the same time as you enjoy the more grandiose environs of Margam Abbey and its large deer-park.

Saint's Well
(Ffynnon-y-Sant).
OS Map 159. GR 386 083.

Travelling north out of the town of Kidwelly (Cidweli) turn just past the old castle onto a road signposted to Ferryside. Take the second left turn to Llansaint, go through the village and just past a chapel on the left called "Tabor" you will locate the well on the left on a bend in the road opposite a narrow lane.

Dedicated to all Saints, whoever they may be, the original well is now capped. At the time this was done a hand pump was installed, necessary probably because Llansaint is situated nearly on the top of a hill and the well was deep. A standing stone at Llangendeirn 12km to the north east is said to be associated with this well in some way.

No cures or tales have been found about this well and it was probably simply a water supply. The water can't be accessed, anyway. None the less it is worth a visit - a nice site, an interesting village and an attractive surrounding area.

* Saint's Well
(Ffynnon-y-Sant).
OS Map 136. GR 049 744.

Marked on the Ordnance Survey map so therefore included. It used to be patronised both by the inmates of the Abbey-Cwm-Hir monastery and any visiting saints, it is said, but the well has either been destroyed or is hidden away close by. The site is supposed to be a few hundred metres off the lane from Llanbister (on the A 483 north of Llandrindod Wells and Bwlch-y-Sarnau). A grove of fir trees now grows there - certain death for any well or spring no matter how historic.

A reliable and knowledgeable local source puts the correct location of this well at GR 053 739 on a slope behind the farmhouse at Esgair-Fawr on private land. It is now used as a water source for the farm and quite a distance from the site marked on the OS map - but we've been caught that way before, haven't we?

* Sarah's Well
(Ffynnon Sarah).
OS Map 116. GR 064 515.

In a small green valley nestling among rolling hills west of the Vale of Clwyd lies Sarah's Well; a venue which well-philes must not allow themselves to miss if anywhere in the vicinity.

The origin of the name is obscure but it might have been that of a popular "priestess" who lived at a nearby cottage, now long gone. Another rumour suggests that it was a sacred well consecrated to St Saran, an Irish saint who did missionary work at Llanynys a few kilometres the other side of Ruthin in the 6th century. We shall probably never really know for sure.

People came from all over to be rid of limb complaints, rheumatism - and unusually, cancerous growths. Total immersion was the rule here, the wealthy being expected to provide a cash contribution for the sustenance of the "priestess" - the poor could get away with a pin. Nobody would be turned away for lack of funds. The well is certainly big enough for total body immersion. Indeed, it is the size of a small garden swimming pool and was quite deep as can be seen from the height of the sill where the water goes out.

To get there, take the B5015 from Ruthin town, signposted for Cerrigydrudion, and travel about 7km to the village of Clawdd-Newydd. Enter the second turning left in the village and go straight for about 2km more. On a left-hand bend just before a bridge over a small brook you will see Sarah's well facing you.

The front is in the shape of a curved stone wall with a gate. A slate plaque set in the wall to one side of the gate bears the well's name. Within, a smooth path suitable for wheelchairs will lead you a mere 10m to the well-side.

You will find yourself in a garden setting of ornamental trees and bushes with grass to sit on among the flowers. The stone seats once provided here for the comfort of supplicants have unfortunately now gone. It is a very attractive setting with the well at its centre. Appreciation must be given to both the present keeper and the local rector who preserved and laid out the site as we see it now, otherwise this well would very likely have been "lost".

The well-pool is large, about 6m by 3m and below ground level in a masonry chamber. At one corner a flight of four stone steps permit an easy descent to the water, the exit for which once allowed the overflow to run into a brook a couple of metres away.

* St Seiriol's Well

(Ffynnon Seiriol).
Festival day 3rd Feb.
OS Maps 114 and 115. GR 631 808.

With brothers in high Welsh places (local kings and princes), it is hardly surprising that when a couple of them founded a monastery at Penmon on Anglesey during the sixth century they installed Seiriol in the top job as the first Abbot. To commemorate his good luck he attached his name to the local spring. How could he do otherwise?

Penmon is almost as far as you can get into the north-east corner of Anglesey. From the west end of the Britannia bridge spanning the Menai Strait, follow the signs into the village of Menai Bridge and then on to Beaumaris along the A525. Carry on the main drag past the interesting castle and the road becomes the B5109. After about 3km turn right into a lane signposted for Penmon and follow this for another 3km to a junction where Penmon is signposted to the left. Don't turn up here but go right in the direction of Penmon Point. Another couple of kilometres will bring you to the old Abbey. Beyond here there is a toll road.

A large car park is located between the imposing, blocky old church dedicated to St Seiriol and a very big masonry dovecote. To get to the well, go along the far side of the car park wall opposite the dovecote, past a small pond and through a doorway in a stone wall. This is about as far as a wheelchair can safely get, but the well is only a few metres further.

It is an attractive location in a sloping grassy courtyard almost like a small quarry. It is probable that stone to build the monastery was obtained here, thus uncovering the spring. The well is in the far corner of the yard - you can't miss it.

A domed structure measuring a couple of metres on a side, it has evidently been added to and refurbished many times over, though most of the original building put up in the eighteenth century still remains. The lower part of the well building and remains of a hermit-type cell or well chapel alongside are estimated to go right back to the age of saints. The cell is said to have been that of St Seiriol himself and it is just possible that the lower section of the well building could be part of the old chapel constructed on the orders of the saint. The site is designated as an ancient monument in the care of the Secretary of State for Wales and has been properly looked after - not like some.

When the rigours of ecclesiastical duty overcame him (as can happen to anyone), Seiriol would spend a bit of time recovering on a small island of 32 hectare close by called Puffin Island (more properly Ynys Seiriol) where there was another monastery. Talk about an island with many names! It is also known as Priestholm, Ynys Glanach and Ennislanach, the last two translating as the Ecclesiastical Island. It is now an SSSI.

The domed well-chamber is high enough to stand up in (about 3m) and 1.5m square. It is said to have last been restored in the 18th century. A ledge goes around three sides with the metre-square well in the centre. The floor-stones overhang the water on two sides and one wall consists of the raw stone face of the quarry. There are three niches on the right, one like a little window and two others facing the door. Of these latter, the one on the left is arched and suggests another entrance used to be there. All niches go deep into the walls. It is still used for wishing (at least) today. At the time of visiting some small white pebbles and coin offerings were noted under the water.

The front of the building was once arched but has since been more enclosed with a brick wall with a rectangular portal.

Outside there is a small courtyard with a low wall and a seat for the weary.

The hermitage, cell or well-chapel is a few metres to the left, again using the quarry face as one wall. Within this oval line of stones on the edge of a small depression in the ground was where Seiriol spent a lot of his time.

It is noticeable how the stones on the approach to the well have been worn down over the ages, no doubt by the feet of pilgrims - and probably the hands and knees of extreme zealots. It emphasises the definite ambience of great antiquity about St Seiriol's well. Some know it as Mary's well (Ffynnon Fair).

St Seiriol's Well
(Ffynnon Seiriol).
OS Map 114. GR 449 842.

Penmon, where Seiriol had his base and Holyhead (Caergybi) where Cybi managed to stay for a while in his eternal wanderings, are both at the furthest opposite ends of Anglesey in an east/west line. Cybi seems to have been an inveterate gossip, always ready to natter away about things religious, and probably other matters too. He became a bosom pal of Seiriol - abbots in arms, as it were.

They used to regularly meet, if the story can be believed, in open countryside at the halfway point across the island just to the east of Llanerchymedd. It would have been quite a long trip for both of them and their retinue. The followers would have to be fed and watered no less than the saints themselves. An assured supply of water, appropriately blessed and consecrated, determined the site of their assembly. Wine or ale simply would not do; it was a long way home for all and drunks are a dead weight.

St Seiriol's Well, Penmon

By the side of a small stream there were two small springs ideally suited for the job. Seiriol claimed one, Cybi the other. Only Seriol's still provides water while Cybi's has dried up, though its probable location can still be made out.

Llanerchymedd is at the junction of the B5111 and B5112. From the village centre take the B5111 to the west then turn into the first road on the left as you approach the outskirts. Follow this lane for about 4km looking for a bridge over a little brook by a farmhouse on the left called "Clorach".

If you stand on the bridge facing east and walk forward a few metres you will see the well on the right close to the road in a field; a simple cube of brickwork topped by a concrete slab about a metre on a side within which is a pool of scummy water. A sill of much older and probably original stone can be seen at the entrance. This was Seiriol's well. He would never have contemplated drinking from it as it is now but in his day it must have been clear and refreshing during a heated bout of theological hair-splitting with the garrulous Cybi.

Directly opposite on the other side of the road is that worthy's own well. The site lies a few metres from both the road and brook near a couple of stunted trees. It has now run dry due to the uncaring works of Man.

Matthew Arnold wrote a poem about "Seiriol the bright and Cybi the Dark" concerning the site of their theological debates. It begins thus:

In the bare midst of Anglesey they show
Two springs which close by one another play.
And "Thirteen hundred years agone" they say,
"Two saints met often where these waters flow."

The Spout
(Y Pistyll).
OS Map 159. GR 676 038.

From the M4 take the A4067 northbound from junction 45 and turn left at the first roundabout. At the next (mini) roundabout turn left then immediately right and follow this road about 4km to Craig-Cefn-Parc. Go through the hillside village to the school and bear right. Y Pistyll is about half a kilometre along on the left just past the phone box.

Included mostly for its peculiarity, it also has a bit of history. It is the best known of a string of domestic wells and springs which follow the line of a coal seam down through the village of Craig-Cefn-Parc. This spring line was the main reason for the original siting of the village at a time when the major coal mines (now long disused) in the deep, narrow valley below were being driven into the hillside. Colliers and their families had to live somewhere and they also had to be provided with a regular supply of fresh water. The spring line was providentially placed.

The one feeding Y Pistyll comes from beneath a large coal seam and emerges from the ground a bit to the left and 30m or so uphill from the pipe and has never been known to run low, let alone dry. A cast iron pipe leading from the spring can be seen to the left of the metre-high outlet pipe which is itself of old cast iron, shaped like an inverted "L" and leaning a bit from when a lorry bumped it at one time. The water discharges into a grating which runs under the front yard of a house downhill, thence into a steep open ditch down to the river far below.

The large house directly above the fountain was built in the 1850s for the general manager of a coal mine which was on the other side of the valley close to the river. He arranged for water from the spring to be piped down all the way to this mine for the benefit of his pit-ponies and colliers but later the pipeline was truncated at the spot you see it now. The water is fresh and clear and still drunk by some of the locals. There is a rumour that the Water Authority may wish to capture this constant supply and divert it into their mains. If this ever happens one hopes that they will be sensitive enough to ensure the overflow is sent down the same pipe and they leave Y Pistyll as it is.

Stinking Well
(Ffynnon Ddrewllyd or Ffynnon Cwm-twrch).
OS Map 160. GR 764 410.

Very easy of access, even for wheelchairs. Travel north up the A4067 from Junction 45 on the M4. After about 16km, at Ystalyfera, turn left on the A4068 up a pleasantly wooded side valley in the direction of Brynamman. Just over half a kilometre up this road look out for the Tafarn Twrch public house and turn left immediately after. Cross the river bridge and take the first turning right at the bottom of a steep hill.

A hundred metres along the track will bring you into a miniature village green. The well is directly in front of you.

Once donated to the village of Cwmtwrch (Valley of the wild boar) by the landowner, a Colonel Gough, this well was tastefully and sensitively refurbished in 1993 by Ystalyfera Community Council with assistance from the Welsh Water Authority and the Prince of Wales Trust.

The immediate frontal area is an open space known as Maes-y-ffynnon which was extensively used in the past by religious groups, union rallies and open-air choir singing by both community and professionally organised parties. The local Eisteddfod was held here every year to choose the best of singing, dancing, poetry and declamation. Huge crowds from neighbouring villages regularly thronged the well environs. Every Whitsun, after the midday meal, all local chapel denominationsuntil recently joined in a procession to the well where an open-air service and communal singing were performed.

Not known to be dedicated to any saint, but nevertheless still renowned far and wide, the strangely-tinted waters flowing rapidly from a pipe into a small bowl certainly live up to their name. The Welsh for the verb "to stink" is drewi and a distinctly pungent pong will immediately be discerned by all visitors with active (or even semi-active) nasal tissues. An analysis of the water has revealed that the well's age-old reputation for medicinal virtue was well-founded.

Sulphur compounds and iron salts predominate, the sulphur being responsible for the smell and its value as an ameliorant for skin troubles as well as being a diuretic. The salts would be of assistance in the treatment of blood disorders and that most common of healing well virtues - rheumatism. The well is fervently alleged to cure "hundreds" of common complaints from arthritis, mouth ulcers, gout and baldness to psoriasis, eczema, neurosis and piles; the only stipulation being that the water must be drunk immediately it is drawn. Failure to do this will result in a loss of all its medicinal powers.

If a bottle of well water is placed in a refrigerator, the smell, and assumedly the potency, will disappear after a couple of days. Boiling the water will result in an unprepossessing dark liquid as the dissolved chemical components join with each other. Right up to the present day many folk drink the waters here, including a large number of the locals. There are a lot of healthy old people in Cwmtwrch.

This is one of the mineral springs which can truly be claimed as having proper healing properties. Why some saint or other did not stake a claim here is a mystery, though it must be said

Stinking Well, Cwmtwrch

that most of the Swansea Valley and its tributaries seem to have been omitted from the missionary Grand Tour. Perhaps the local tribes were a bunch of tough cookies too pagan for even the most fervent of converter.

Whatever the reason, this well is not considered "sacred". It is definitely worth a visit if you are in the vicinity.

* St Sulien's Well
(Ffynnon Sulien).
Feast Day May 13th.
OS Map 125. GR 068 442.

This well is a fine example in the garden of a cottage of the same name. It is suspected that near the site of the ancient chapel of Rug (pron. Reeg) close by was the original place where Sulien (pron. Seel-yen) put down his local Christian roots. There is merit in this theory, if only for the fact it is situated within easy walking distance of the well over dry ground - quite a different proposition from where the present church is dedicated to St Sulien and St Mael.

This church is situated at Corwen on the opposite bank of the fast and deep river Dee where there has been a ford for millennia, but it would have been impossible for Sulien to get to his well in an emergency from there if the river was only a little bit in flood - as often happens during the winter. It is a pretty little church tucked out of the way behind the Owain Glyndwr hotel overlooking the central town square and is well worth a visit. So is Rug, now a small private chapel built in the 15th century and open to the public at times during summer.

Inseparable chums Sulien and Mael, so it is said, but poor old St Mael didn't get a local well dedicated to him; at least not one which has survived. They both came over from France with a bunch of other missionaries, liked it in Wales and stayed.

Sulien, cousin to St David and Confessor, founded many churches throughout Wales including that at Llandyssul (he was sometimes known as Tysul) where he also had a sacred well. To find the well under discussion go west along the A5 from Corwen and turn right at the traffic lights on to the A494 just over a kilometre from the town. Rug chapel will be seen on the left and after another half kilometre there will be the first turning to the right. Ffynnon Sulien is down there. It is not recommended to take a car down this track but the cottage is only 100m from the road, anyway, and was once on the route of the local heritage trail. The well was said to be good for rheumatism and many other problems

* Taffs Well
(Ffynnon Daf).
OS Map 171. GR 121 835.

Also called Ffynnon Dwym, this spa-well was famous before, during and since the time of the Roman invasion. If you leave the M4 at Junction 31 and travel north along the A470 past the storybook Castell Goch high on the cliff to your right (strongly recommended for a visit after you see the well), leave the dual-carriageway at the first exit and follow the signs to Taffs Well.

Going through the village, look at for the Taffs Well public house on the left and descend the steep path alongside into the village park. The well is over to your left as you approach the river bank; an attractive masonry building built into the side of the levee which holds back the raging River Taf during times of high flood.

Access to the healing waters, unfortunately, is barred. A locked door prohibits entry to the building and nothing can be seen through the windows without a powerful torch. Before the area was "improved", anyone could go there to be cured of rheumatism or lameness within four weeks of bathing.

The Romans are said to have built a surround to contain the substantial waters welling up from the ground. Traces of a masonry wall dating from this time are supposed to be buried under the levee. The well was in use continually from then on and when corrugated iron sheeting was locally invented an enclosed bath house was erected. Regular users were expected to contribute financially for upkeep and repair.

When a man occupied the premises he would hang a pair of trousers outside - an old pair, taken especially for the purpose; if a prankster then stole them he would still be able to preserve his tender modesty and dignity on the journey home. Females would likewise hang out a garment positively identifiable as female. The message was the same in either case - "All members of the other gender keep out!" During this era, youngsters would gather at the well on the seventh Sunday after every Easter to splash each other with water and dance until evening.
The ghost of a tall, slender lady dressed in grey is said to haunt the well. Who she was and why she picked on Taffs Well is not known. On stormy nights it is whispered that her wails and groans of torment can clearly be heard emanating from the direction of the well, especially just after stop-tap at the nearby taverns.

Alas for such innocent times! The well was subsequently replaced with a more permanent and soulless concrete structure which became vandalised and unkempt until the present cover was erected when the height of the levee was raised in recent times.

Tegid's Well
(Ffynnon Degid).
OS Map125. GR (centre point) 910 335.

The biggest alleged well chamber you are likely to see and also the largest natural body of water in Wales, plunging to depths of over 40m. It is Bala Lake (Llyn Tegid), home to Wales' answer to the Loch Ness monster - a fearsome, rarely-seen creature which has been cursed with the absurd and unflattering nick-name of "Teggie".

Somewhere at the bottom is said to lie the remains of a fine palace belonging to a certain King Tegid (probably a Roman exile more correctly called Tacitus) who was fond of the good life. Feasts, music and singing competitions were regularly held at the behest of this noble, royal personages attending from far and wide. He was also a great big slob; a cruel and arrogant ruler who persecuted his tenants beyond all reason.

One day he sent word to an elderly harpist who lived among the Arenig mountains to the north. The famous musician was respectfully requested to attend a feast to celebrate the arrival of the king's first-born and play for the delight of other guests. Old though he was, the harpist agreed to make the trip and arrived, tired and hungry, at a bluff overlooking the palace nestling in the green vale below.

It was near sunset and he thought he would rest a while before making the descent. In a nearby bush a blackbird (a Welsh blackbird - he could tell by the accent) began to sing its evening song. The musician was entranced at the sweetness of the melody and could not move for fear of disturbing this singer which could create such music so far superior to the harsh sounds made by the crude instruments of Man. It became dark; the harpist slept.

Morning sunlight woke him. All was still except for the plash of rippling water. He arose, the aches and pains of elderly joints and muscles unused to a hard bed immediately forgotten at the sight before him.

A mighty lake filled the valley. King Tegid and his palace had been claimed by the water-fairies who had opened the portals of Ffynnon Gower on the opposite side of the valley to get rid of Tegid and his brutal enforcers. Legend has it that a similar fate will also overcome the present town of Bala one day.

A rather more complex variation states that Tegid would often hear the words "Vengeance" and "Revenge" being called from afar - probably his conscience berating him for his cruelty. When the old harpist arrived the feast began and during the interval the musician heard the beat of small wings and the same dire words. He looked around and saw a blackbird hovering, staring intently at him and beckoning him to follow. How a bird could do this is not clear but the harpist understood and followed the winged messenger out of the palace, up the hill and into the woods. The bird flew away.

The harpist tried to retrace his steps back to the palace but got lost and fell asleep from exhaustion. He awoke to see the lake and his harp floating ashore to ground on the grass at his feet.

Of course, they're only legends after all. Aren't they?

* St Tegla's Well
(Ffynnon Degla).
OS Map 116. GR 194 523.

The well dedicated to St Tegla, a Welsh saint who probably lived in the 5th century, is in the village of Llandegla and the church there is also in her name. To reach it you must turn north-west up the A5104 at its junction with the A525 and turn left a couple of hundred metres from the junction. The church will be on your right nearly at the far end of the village.

Facing the church is a row of four attractive old houses. To the right of this row a gravelled track will take you through a farmyard (public footpath). At the far end will be a field and stile. If you keep to the right of the field, following the course of the River Alyn (a sacred river name in Wales), a walk of only 100m will bring you to the well. The total distance from the road to the well is less than 250m overall and generally level.

The well may be a bit hard to spot among the trees but look for the gleam of water and two trees which have their roots entangled and grow in the shape of a V. It is roughly triangular in shape - about a metre wide, half as much again in length and half a metre deep. The hewn masonry walls rise to ground level; the water coming from beneath a large slab at the wide end of the pool. Water exits underneath the roots of one of the twin trees to flow into the River Alyn only a few metres away.

A lot went on at this well. It was once believed to be good for curing diseases of the brain for which the patient had to bathe and sit in the water for some time then go to the church to pray for a cure. Payment was made in the form of either cash being left at the well - not in it - towards parish funds or the offering (and acceptance) of a rooster (live - not cooked) to the local clergy. Wishing and divination were also practiced here with the usual bits of white rock or pins.

Epilepsy was the speciality though, the ritual for which probably went back to long before the Age of Saints because of its unmistakable overtones of magic. The sufferer would have to take a rooster (a woman took a hen) to the well after dark on a Friday or Saturday, bathe his limbs in the water and walk slowly around the well three times carrying the rooster and muttering the Lord's Prayer. Then came the nasty bit.

The unfortunate fowl would be pricked with a pin until blood appeared and was then thrown into the well. Some sort of container would have to be used for this, obviously, as legging it through the woods on a dark night in frantic pursuit of a sore and dripping specimen of angry poultry is not everyone's idea of a good time. Cash would then be left at the well and the pin dropped in.

Repairing to the church, he would go round this three times carrying the rooster and doing the same mumble as he went before entering and donating more cash into the alms chest. He would sleep there using a Bible as a pillow, rising before dawn to blow breath into the rooster's face in order to transfer the disease. Yet more cash would find its way into the alms chest. The supplicant would then head for home leaving his wet, shivering and resentful feathered friend behind. If the rooster disappeared, relief from the complaint was assured.

The clergy of that time were noted for their fondness for white meat. It would be surprising indeed if the bribe remained in the church for very long. Custodians of Llandegla parish church would not only have been pretty wealthy but quite well-fed (forgive the pun) into the bargain.

St Teilo's Well

(Ffynnon Deilo).
Festival Day 9th February.
OS Map 145. GR 101 271.

Poor old Teilo didn't have much luck with the survival of his other wells, as the entries below will show. Perhaps the most famous, and definitely the one about which most is known, also seems to be the most forgotten.

There is no doubt about the pagan importance of this spring; the immediate surroundings still seem to impart an aura of primitive associations. Whether it is in the lie of the land or the subtle moulding of the surface soil which, even though it has been altered somewhat for agricultural reasons and way off the beaten track, gives the distinct impression it has been used over and over again by numberless generations.

As indeed it has. From the time the old church dedicated to St Teilo (now a ruin) was founded close by, this spring not only increased in importance but also gave rise to rituals, some semi-pagan in nature, and stories which persisted until relatively recent times - after the Great War, in fact.

But all that has now gone; the place is virtually a ruin, like the church. This can only be explained by the general loss of interest in certain parts of out heritage and the fact that the location is rather remote and can be hard to locate. However, a public footpath is still shown running to the well on the Ordnance Survey map and it is only a matter of 150m from a properly paved lane.

It is part of a short spring-line and not so long ago a fine stone enclosure impounded the issue from the largest spring. The outflow from this tipped into a fair-sized pond and thence down through a field to a brook. Only a neglected shadow of the pond can still be seen. The old wall which once retained the water to a reasonable depth still stands but the water level had been greatly lowered to leave a muddy area absolutely smothered with weeds - an extremely unpleasant state for such a famous well to be in. The pond appears to have been at least 20m long by 7m wide when full.

Cattle seemed to like drinking there (it could have been on one of the Drovers routes) because another name by which the spring is known is Ffynnon-yr-Ychen (Spring of the Oxen). This probably came about after the pond was constructed.

Legend has it that in 560AD, when St Teilo lay upon his death-bed at Llandeilo monastery in the Towy Valley, he imparted strict instructions that his skull was to be parted from the rest of him after a period of a year when his bones had been stripped of flesh by the creatures of the grave. This token cranium was then to be taken to the place which had given him most pleasure during his life - the Pembrokeshire Llandeilo. It appears that no suggestion was made about what to do with the skull on delivery (though one version of the story does state that it be used for healing), but Welsh country folk are nothing if not enterprising. Pilgrims to the well were thereafter informed that the only way to obtain maximum benefit from the water was to drink it from Teilo's brain pan, at a small extra fee, of course.

Lung problems including TB and whooping cough, all once common ailments, were said to be the special curative attributes of the waters though any disease would benefit in some measure.

This practice is said to have continued until the early 19th century and it was revived during the First World War when people came to the well to pray for an end to the terrible fighting. It is rather unlikely St Teilo's head-bone would have lasted so long and one could be forgiven for darkly wondering where the custodians of the well obtained the successors to the original. A similar story to this exists at some other revered wells throughout the world.

But this one is in need of regular visitors to renew its former importance and hopefully it may one day be restored. From the A40 at Narberth go north along the B4313 to Maenclochog and turn right by the post office opposite the church. In a few hundred metres, at the bottom of the first dip in the road, turn right and travel for nearly 2km to the first left, signposted for Llanycefn. Don't turn down here but carry on another 150m to the next house on the left called Maes Ffynnon. Opposite this house is a field gate which is the start of the short footpath shown on the OS map. If you keep to the hedge on the left, the well is at the far end of the field on the right in a grove of short scraggy trees.

St Teilo's Well
(Ffynnon Deilo).
OS Map 171. GR 156 780.

If you stand at the roadside facing the entrance of the famous cathedral at Llandaff in Cardiff, the old Bishop's palace will be on your right at the eastern end of the High Street. Walk towards the palace and turn left down a steep narrow lane.

St Teilo's well is in the wall on your left only a few metres down the hill.

It has now run dry because of all the tarmac and dense housing in the locality which does not allow sufficient rain to soak into the ground. Even in Teilo's day there was not much of a flow. As befits the second bishop of Llandaff in the 6th century he would not have wanted to go very far for a drink of water and this well was nice and convenient to consecrate whether he was staying at his digs or working hard in the original church which he shared with a couple of other saints.

Now little more than a grill in the wall allowing a view of the inside, it is still worth a visit when you come here to walk around the fine cathedral which Teilo would have given his best socks to preach in.

* St Teilo's Well
(Ffynnon Deilo).

There is another well dedicated to St Teilo near the village of Pendoylan on OS Map 170. GR 063 759. Unfortunately it is on private land and difficult of access though a public footpath is marked on the map running close by.

*St Tewdrick's Well
(Ffynnon Tewderick).
Festival day, April 1st.
OS Map 172 GR 523 912.

Had a full life, did St Tewdrick. He was, apparently, King of Glamorgan and ruled benevolently. It wasn't easy being a king in those days, but Tewdrick lived to a fair old age, packed in his job and left home to spend a well-earned retirement at Tintern as a hermit not far from the Abbey. He wasn't there long before a bunch of Saxon thugs who broke into south Wales in 577AD began wreaking havoc in his former kingdom.

The situation got a bit too much for his successor, his son Meurig, to handle and he sent for Tewdrick's assistance. The old warrior responded magnificently, snorting furiously through his greying whiskers he grabbed his trusty sword, rallied the troops and plunged into battle close to Tintern. He should have known better at his age. He received a mortal wound and asked to be buried on the small island of Flatholm (Ynys Hafren) in the upper Severn estuary

He didn't make it. Close to the coast, the draft beasts (oxen or stags, depending on who you ask) pulling his cart stopped abruptly and stubbornly refused to go any further. Perhaps the beasts knew their cargo was close to death because their stopping place was right by a spring of clear water. (Another story is that the spring commenced to flow when the cart stopped at the location). Tewdrick was removed from the cart and his faithful servants washed his wounds in the spring. Tewdrick drew his last breath by that spring. His son, at Tewdrick's last request, built a church as a shrine close by among the trees and there the grand old man was buried. The nearby village of Pwllmeyric is named after the son who was also made a saint and said to have had his own well dedicated there.

The well was restored to its present tidy condition in 1977 by the former Monmouth District Council. The date of Tewdrick's death is given on the plaque as 470AD, yet other "authorities" insist the correct year was 595AD. Whatever the truth, Tewdrick was made a Saint and Martyr for his holy endeavours.

The water is below ground level and quite clear. A surround has been put up and another fence around this because the shape and depth could be dangerous for children or local drunks. Steps lead down to the water. The well is still used today by those who value its undoubted virtue

Trefriw Roman Spa
(Ffynnon Rufeinig).
OS Map 115. GR 778 653.

The name of Trefriw village is made up of two Welsh words, one archaic, and signifies "Town of Healing". This is appropriate since it lies close to the famous Spa on the western side of the Conway valley at the edge of the great Carneddau massif and received the name as a direct result of this proximity.

From the A55 express-way on the north Wales coast, branch off into Conway town and follow the B5106 for about 12km then look out for a large grey reception building on the right a

205

little way past the village of Dolgarrog.

As far as is known there was no natural spring here until a quarry and mine was started so no pagan of religious connection can be made. 5km to the north on the valley floor lie preserved the ruins of a Roman fort called Caerhun where the 20th Roman legion had its base of operations. The Romans were ever greedy for metals to fuel their mighty war machine and when traces of lead, copper, silver, gold and zinc ores were located in the vicinity they press-ganged a load of local slaves to do all the hard work and started them digging.

At least that's the story. Whatever the truth of it, somewhere around this time the mineral properties of natural springs tapped in the exposed rock were noted and the place turned into a therapeutic bath (for wounded soldiers, perhaps?). The baths hewn from the solid rock are still there.

Over the years it became famous and was used for healing long after the Romans left the Welsh in a much better condition than they found them and went back home.

In the 1700s a proper bath house was built and when the Age of the Spa took off yet another erected in 1874 to accommodate the large and growing number of visitors. The village of Trefriw (be sure to visit the quality woollen mill here) used to be the highest navigable point on the River Conway in those days; sea-going ships jamming the old quay, now neglected, to take on cargoes of metals, timber and slate. Said to be the furthest inland port in Wales, paddle steamers and other pleasure boats from the coastal resorts of Llandudno, Deganwy and Conway landed up to 1,000 trippers a day to sample the local delights of climbing, angling, painting and other pastimes - many going on by coach to the Spa.

Trefriw Spa Wells, near Llanrwst

The building of a railway finished off the port status of Trefriw but the Spa was still well patronised. Inevitably, as the Spa craze declined, so did the fortunes of Trefriw and it was eventually abandoned until the 1980s when a brave entrepreneur began to resurrect the place. Since then the complex has improved beyond measure, far surpassing its former glory. Assisted by exports of the iron and sulphur-rich waters, the reception building has been converted into a small but extremely fine shop where one can purchase health and beauty products based on minerals found in the waters and there is also a restaurant of equal quality where visitors can obtain tasty snacks and light meals. Although the baths themselves are not at present available to bathe in, a very informative self-guiding tour with push-button voice boxes and appropriate sound effects is offered at a small fee which will take you through the history of the site, the bath houses and the well grotto where the springs come to the surface.

The chalybeate and sulphur content is said to be of the highest concentration found in Wales and all the waters tapped here have unquestioned and proven medical properties. Those suffering particularly from depression, anaemia, skin diseases or certain types of heart problems will certainly derive some benefit from these waters. It is also rumoured to alleviate "female complaints" - whatever they are.

Outside is a formal "wishing well" in the shape of a low fountain, the donations from which are given to the Great Ormond Street Hospital for Sick Children. Please be generous if you use this facility.

St Trillo's Well

(Ffynnon Drillo).
Festival Day 15th June.
OS Map 116. GR 842 812.

There are many Welsh folk who still assert that the epic hero Madoc ap Owain Gwynedd was the first European to find America. Indeed, who can definitely prove otherwise? But why did he not publicise the fact more widely?

Of course, it's quite possible that his landfall was in the region of what was to become the Bronx and he suddenly had a vision of what the distant future would be like there. If this were the case no-one could possibly criticise him for keeping his mouth firmly shut.

That was over 800 years ago and he chose a small promontory on the north Wales coast to debark on his marathon voyage - a location that had been important for religious reasons for centuries before that. It is Rhos Point near Colwyn Bay.

St Trillo, a Celtic missionary and later an abbot, started it all in the 6th century. He caused a well-chapel to be built over the top of a natural spring which he asserted had "holy" properties. There is still a chapel there today, not the original one but extremely old for all that.

It is a tiny place, just big enough to hold up to eight people with seating for six. Holy Communion services are held there every Friday at 8.00am and it is open to the public during the daytime. Measuring 5m by 3m and a bit less than 3m high, it is entered through a narrow vaulted wooden door to the whitewashed interior. The floor is of cobbles and at the far end is a stone altar table standing over the well itself which is in a sunken chamber 1.5m long and half a metre wide. A metal grid and a couple of removable wooden planks give access to the water.

St Trillo's Well, Rhos-on-Sea

Clear and still is the water, a little step halfway along providing a maximum depth of maybe half a metre. Coins and small white pebbles are offered by many visitors who also leave messages and supplication written on scraps of paper on the altar; requests for divine intervention or assistance, some of which are poignant, others truly heartbreaking to read. It is nice to see visible proof that surviving wells and springs can still give hope and comfort to some.

To the right are a couple of wall niches which once held communal drinking vessels for the use of the many who came here seeking cures for sickness and disease. Monks from a nearby abbey used to pray here for success at the fish trap they built on the shore a short distance away.

Above the well chamber is a tiny stained-glass window in fine primary colours depicting St Trillo in a suitable saintly pose and to the left is a further to another local saint - St Eilian - whose well, also local, was disgracefully treated not so long ago (see entry on St Eilian's well). This latter window exhibits a strange illusion which may be seen from several angles depending upon the strength of light shining through the glass. The rich, intense blue of the saint's cloak produces a very convincing 3-D effect which can cause the eyes to twist in an attempt to rationalise what is seen.

Outside, twin sturdy buttresses with a seat between them face out over the sea, and the immediate area is fenced off. The location of the chapel can be a bit hard to spot if you don't know exactly where it is to start with.

On the sea-front at Rhos-on-sea, west of Colwyn Bay, head west along the promenade from the Rhos Abbey hotel, past the ancient building once used by monks (now Rhos Fynach Tavern) and in a couple of hundred metres look out for Trillo Avenue on your left. Carry on a bit more and you will see a section of low stone wall on the right surmounted by a simple board announcing the existence of the Parish of Llandrillo. The little chapel is below this wall and easily reached by a short paved path from the road.

St Trillo was buried on Bardsey Island.

* St Trillo's Well
(Ffynnon Drillo).
OS Map 125. GR 032 375.

At Llandrillo in the upper Dee valley and only included because it is still on the Ordnance Survey map.

From the church in the village, travel west along the B4401 a couple of hundred metres to the first field gate on the right, alongside the entrance to the Tyddyn Llan Hotel.

The well used to be on the right in the next field further away from the road but all that is left is a shallow depression in the ground only supplying a trickle of water in wet years and now more of a seepage than a spring.

Before the middle of the 19th century it was said to be in a different field by an ancient stone altar (pagan connections? - almost certainly) but when the farmer stopped pilgrims attending the site it dried up and resurfaced where it is now, altar and all. This was believed to be St Trillo's doing. Another story is that it ceased to flow because a dead cat or dog was thrown in it.

* Trinity Well
(Fynnon y Drindod).
OS Map 170. GR 937 737.

From the village of Pentremeyric on the A48 west of Cowbridge travel south on the B4268 to the junction with the A4270 (about 4km) and turn right at the cross-roads. A journey of another 4km through another cross-roads will bring you into the pretty village of Llandow (Llandw).

Go past the ancient church dedicated to the Holy Trinity and turn right just before the railway bridge into a cul-de-sac called "Ty Draw". Follow this for a couple of hundred metres to the end at a railway crossing. There is not much further to go. If the railway line is crossed, the spring will be found at the end of the second field on the left of the railway line at the bottom of a shallow vale. A trickle of water flows under the railway embankment here and if this is followed to its source (a matter of only a few metres) the spring will be located. The water from here forms part of the beginnings of the River Alun - a name with important religious associations in Wales.

At present, Ffynnon-y-Drindod is a pool approximately 10m by 4m and up to a metre deep. It is mostly filled with water plants and has been impounded with an earth bank to serve as a drinking place for farm animals. Around the pool erratically worn earth terraces and platforms bear witness to much human use in the past. On the uphill side some ruined masonry can just be discerned under a bramble patch from where the water probably once issued from the earth.

At one time, long ago, it was evidently a properly cared-for well which was heavily frequented and held in high esteem for curing the crippled and those suffering from many types of eczema and other diseases of the skin.

It is sad to see it in its present state, this place to which pilgrims and the sick once flocked. An air of melancholy permeates the immediate surroundings, due no doubt to the loss of its former prominence. Perhaps some day it will be redeemed from this unhappy state for the delight of all those well-wishers who wish wells well.

Trinity Spa Wells
(Ffynnonhau Drindod).
OS Map 147. GR 056 608.

On the eastern end of the mid-Wales "Spa Belt" stands the town of Llandrindod Wells, once more returning to prominence with its own working spa. The Church of the Holy Trinity, to which the town owns its name, was built on a bluff above the famous wells which have been used since pagan times, and almost certainly before.

It was an important medical centre in the minds of the many thousands of sufferers who came here each year. Large hotels installed their own pump rooms and treatment centres to capitalise on the trade but the original spa remained and was restored in the early 1980s by the Llandrindod Wells Spa Town Trust. More recently it has been greatly improved and now operates as a noted complementary medicine centre as well as a spa.

It is in the Rock Park, only a short distance from the shopping centre. To find it go northbound into the town along the A483 and turn left at the first main cross-roads. A signpost will show the way and the turning right at this point will lead to the lake. Follow the one-way road past the church on the left, turn left at the end and over the railway bridge. At a roundabout you will see a pedestrian entrance to the park on the left but go a bit further and vehicular access will be on the same side.

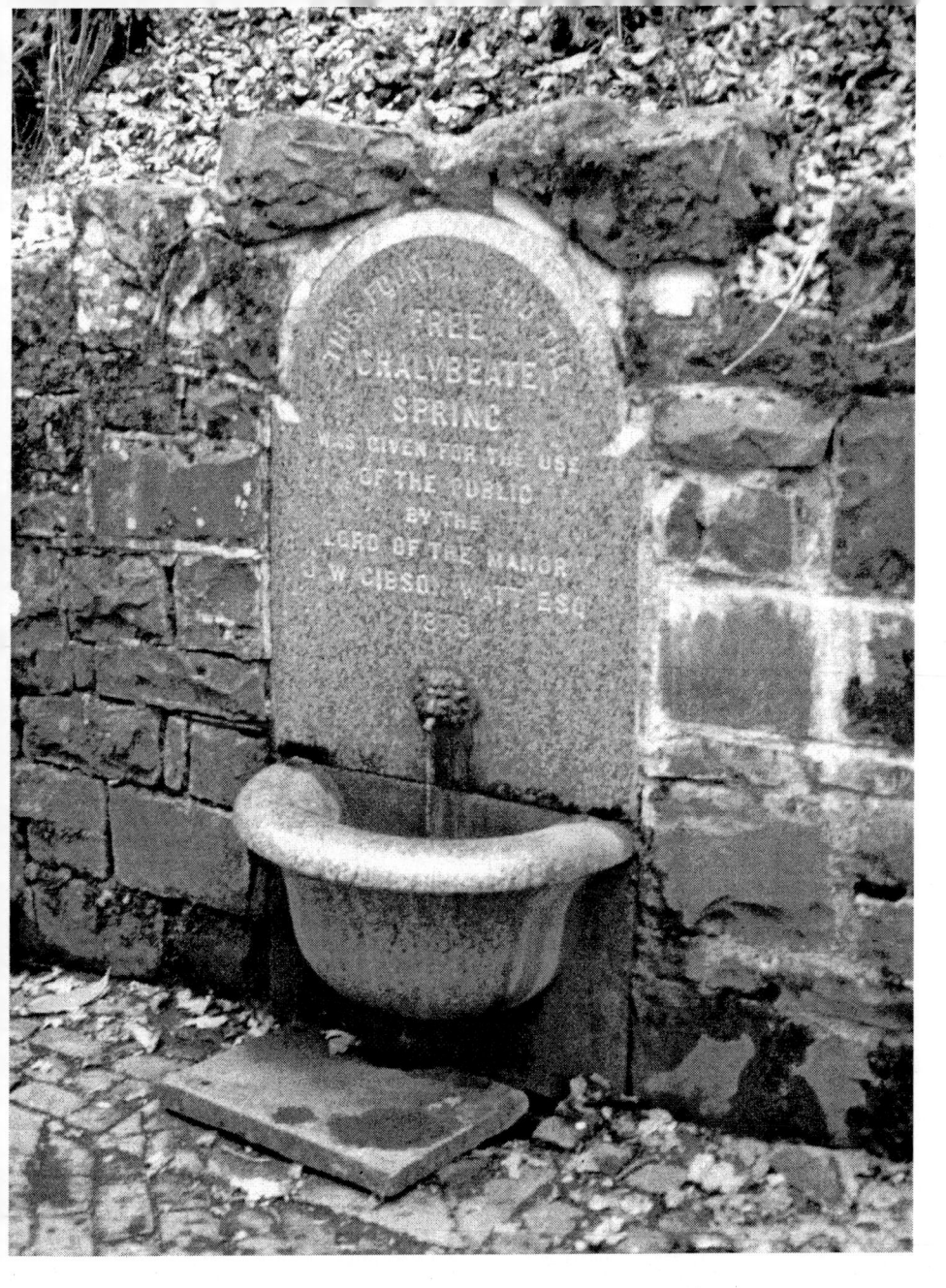

Chalybeat Spring, Llandridod Wells

Rock Park is an attractive wooded area latticed with paved paths suitable for a wheelchair. The spacious Spa buildings are in the centre not far from the road. Entrance to the reception area is open to the public and shows a display of the history of the spa. Many water-related treatments were prescribed here in its heyday including electric therapies and massage. Today many more are offered; reflexology, aromatherapy, acupuncture, hypno-analysis, homeopathy, to name but a few.

Five different sorts of mineralised water were once available; sulphur, chalybeate, saline, radium and magnesium, all of which are recognised as helpful for the relief of certain ailments. To sufficiently dissolve some of these elements, the water could have lain in deep rock strata for up to millions of years from the time it fell as rain on the surrounding hills.

A small stream, the overflow from the town lake, cuts through the park close by and if you follow this 50m or so upstream from the spa buildings you will come to the chalybeate spring. It is a little red marble structure set in a wall at the side of the path and was erected for the use of the town population in 1879 by a local dignitary. A spout projecting from a small metal lion's head set in the marble allows a trickle of water heavy with iron and other salts into a bowl.

Those desirous of attending any of the divers treatments offered by this worthy enterprise are invited to contact the Llandrindod Wells Complementary Health Centre on 01597 822997.

St Tudno's Well

(Ffynnon Dudno).
Festival Day 6th June.
OS Map 115. GR 771 838.

The well-conscious visitor to the popular resort of Llandudno may find it rather peculiar that the well of the saint after whom the town was named is hardly acknowledged at all. But it does still exist.

To be fair, it's not the fault of the local administration. They have done a superb job of providing direction signs to places of interest around the town - except for one to Tudno's well. The reason for this omission is all too familiar to those interested in such places.

In common with so many other terribly neglected wells and springs in the Principality, St Tudno's old watering hole is on private land; but only just - and that's the tragedy.

To find the location you must ascend the steep road towards the summit of the Great Orme, following the tramline, and turn right where it flattens out half a kilometre from the top.

A signpost will direct you to St Tudno's church at this point. Follow the narrow road down to the neat but plain old church and alongside the graveyard wall until you reach a sharp left-hand bend. There is a pull-in a little way further on opposite the church.

Just above that sharp bend in the road a footpath goes uphill following a barbed-wire fence. St Tudno's well is about 50m or so up this path on the left beyond a thicket of thorn bushes - and completely out of sight. Although only a few metres outside the country park area, this well is effectively out of bounds to the public.

It is such a shame. The Great Orme being nothing more than a big block of porous limestone, it is rare to find a spring near the top which is why this one was so important to old Tudno in the 6th century when he built his church on the site occupied by the existing one. Downhill from the spring a small square reservoir fed by the same aquifer will be seen in the field and this was used to supply part of the town with water. So the spring still has some use even today.

St Tudno was a Welsh hermit who resided in a cave (Ogof Llech) on the great Orme. He is known to be buried somewhere on Bardsey Island.

Village Well near Bodelwyddan
OS Map 116. GR 983 762.

The village of Bodelwyddan's main claim to fame is the elegant "marble church" - impossible to miss when travelling on the A55 dual carriageway between St Asaph and Abergele.

The practical service well a short distance away has no proper history, no sacred or pagan connections and no known curative powers yet it is worthy of mention due to the curiosity of its construction. In outline it is reminiscent of the better-known church just down the road on which the builder probably modelled it.

Built in the latter part of the 19th century to serve a row of estate houses close by, the whole thing is about 5m high and 1.5m round with a cone-shaped roof supported by very old, crooked and weathered timbers. It is now capped for safety reasons but a small overflow issues from the chamber to end up in a drain.

Using the marble church as both a landmark and starting point, go west a couple of kilometres along the course of the old A55 (not the dual carriageway) to a short row of grey stone semis on the right. A stone wall on the left will be concealing the dual carriageway. At the end of the row of houses the well should be seen at the roadside tucked into a corner by a right-hand turning.

* Whitewell
(Ffynnon Wen).
OS Map 158. GR 09/99

Included only because it is marked on the Ordnance Survey map. It seems to have disappeared from the location shown and is very likely a victim of land drainage. A bit further down the muddy lane passing the field where the well should be, and a few metres beyond a low railway bridge, there is a little brick well on the left side of the lane but it is a very poor thing and surely not the original Whitewell.

St Winifred's Well
(Ffynnon Gwenfrewi).
Festival Day 3rd November.
OS Map 116. GR 185 763.

Arguably one of the most important, and certainly the best documented well in Wales, St Winifred's has been a place of veneration since long before Christian times.

Flowing from a cleft in the limestone at the head of a narrow valley not far from the sea, the sheer volume of water would have ensured its importance even without the undoubted healing qualities it possesses. Hundreds of thousands, perhaps millions of pilgrims throughout the ages can't all be wrong.

It is also the biggest and best preserved in Wales; even a casual study of the differing styles, types and sizes of masonry work making up the existing buildings exhibiting the strong desire to keep this sacred place presentable at almost any cost. Work on adapting and refurbishing the structures has been going on ever since they were erected in the beginning of the 16th century. The overall effect is that of a tasteful and integrated patchwork.

Before that time a succession of more primitive chapels stood on the same site. The name of the town which evolved to service the needs of pilgrims is Holywell: it couldn't be anything else, when you think about it.

It is located at the bottom of the hill from Holywell on the B5121 heading for Greenfield and quite difficult to miss. A nominal charge is levied for access to the complex which consists of a lawned courtyard, a large outdoor bath the size of a swimming pool, the inner shrine of the well-chapel and a shop.

Legend would have us believe that the spring gushed forth when the gentle and very beautiful maiden Winifred was decapitated there by a local noble, a certain Prince Caradoc, whose odious carnal advances she had quite correctly spurned. Princes were always doing nasty things like that in those days. St Beuno, her uncle, who just happened to be close enough to witness the foul deed, replaced her head and brought her back to life. He was familiar with this technique, apparently, as he is said to have performed it at other places (see Digwg's Well). Almost as an afterthought, in one modification of the story he punished Prince Caradoc by making him sink slowly into the earth.

The water is of quite exceptional volume by Welsh standards and strongly impregnated with calcium and iron salts with many other trace elements. Stones in the well stained by the

St Winifred's Well, Hollywell

iron are said to be the drops of blood scattered by the hapless maiden as she fell. The spring surfaces in the inner pool of the chapel. It is over a metre in depth and contained within a star-shaped wall on three sides with fluted pillars flanking the pool and ascending to an interesting and complex vaulted ceiling. Effigies of St Winifred, St Beuno and others are many; a particularly interesting feature being the decoration along the upper part outside the well-chapel which mostly depicts carvings of animals with a few human faces thrown in for good measure.

No other Welsh well is known to be definitely dedicated to St Winifred yet so revered was it that even during the religious pogrom of the Reformation it was seen as such a useful source of revenue from the multitudes of pilgrims that it was more or less left alone. Lust for money has always bred hypocrisy. Set against that was the fact that the well had apparently been the cause of very many cures - a situation which still exists today. No religious intolerance could possibly justify denying the masses of such a valuable medical asset.

Not that a spirit of theological peace and harmony prevailed. Oh no! Various Protestant groups attempted vandalisms, underground groups of Catholics met in dingy local taverns. Subterfuge and intrigue was rife and the well still attracted supplicants from all walks of society and religious persuasions.

It is still extremely popular except, apparently, for Royalty. The last known Royal to make a proper pilgrimage there was James the Second in 1686 who came in a proper spirit of reverent humility. Services are still held there. Mass baptisms, individual and group devotions and sufferers who come in the hope of being healed are often observed. Between the well-chamber and the outer pool is a narrow slot flanked by steps and fitted with a hand rail. It is about 1.5m deep and those unable to walk are carried through on the backs of able-bodied volunteers - a practice carried on ever since wells were first used for healing. An old carving in the well chamber testifies to this.

St Beuno's Stone lays in one corner of the outer pool and folk still kneel on this whilst performing their own personal devotions and rituals. Candles for both remembrance and offering by the sick and healthy alike burn on a rack by the well and a hand-pump provides water direct from the source spring.

All in all, St Winifred's well cannot be treated as anything but a truly sacred place for anyone with the slightest shred of spiritual feeling. When you make a trip to north Wales be sure not to miss the experience.

* Witch's Well ?
(Ffynnon y Wrach).
OS Map 114. GR 224 823.

Travelling on the road from Holyhead towards the spectacular scenery of the South Stack, about a kilometre past the last of the town houses, a peculiar structure will be seen in a field on the left close to the roadside.

About 5m high, octagonal walls support a hemispherical roof. Access to the interior is barred by a gate for the safety of farm animals, but details can easily be seen. Inside, the chamber is quite circular and 4m in diameter, the brick-lined well in the centre, also circular, is about a metre in diameter and surrounded by a paved walkway. The water can just be seen about a metre below the lip of the well. On the right-hand side a set of steps descends into a small secondary chamber. No water flows to or from this well.

Reliable information regarding the history of Witch's Well has proven almost impossible to obtain to date though the name itself is significant, pointing to ancient pagan use of the spring rather than Christian. At some Welsh "sacred" wells communion with Satan was believed to be possible by filling the mouth with water, making horrible faces at the well then spitting the water out with as much realistic loathing as the applicant's thespian powers would permit. A curse of personal choice would then be uttered. Do this procedure three times and the Evil One was supposed to come on line in some manner. What the next step should be is not clear. Could Witch's Well be one of these places, one wonders, or did a noted local witch once live close by?

Mean Ddu Well, Brecon

FREE DETAILED CATALOGUE

Capall Bann is owned and run by people actively involved in many of the areas in which we publish. A detailed illustrated catalogue is available on request, SAE or International Postal Coupon appreciated. **Titles can be ordered direct from Capall Bann, post free in the UK** (cheque or PO with order) or from good bookshops and specialist outlets.

A Breath Behind Time, Terri Hector
Angels and Goddesses - Celtic Christianity & Paganism, M. Howard
Arthur - The Legend Unveiled, C Johnson & E Lung
Auguries and Omens - The Magical Lore of Birds, Yvonne Aburrow
Asyniur - Womens Mysteries in the Northern Tradition, S McGrath
Beginnings - Geomancy, Builder's Rites & Electional Astrology in the European Tradition, Nigel Pennick
Between Earth and Sky, Julia Day
Book of the Veil, Peter Paddon
Caer Sidhe - Celtic Astrology and Astronomy, Vol 1, Michael Bayley
Caer Sidhe - Celtic Astrology and Astronomy, Vol 2 M Bayley
Call of the Horned Piper, Nigel Jackson
Cat's Company, Ann Walker
Celtic Faery Shamanism, Catrin James
Celtic Lore & Druidic Ritual, Rhiannon Ryall
Celtic Sacrifice - Pre Christian Ritual & Religion, Marion Pearce
Celtic Saints and the Glastonbury Zodiac, Mary Caine
Circle and the Square, Jack Gale
Compleat Vampyre - The Vampyre Shaman, Nigel Jackson
Creating Form From the Mist - The Wisdom of Women in Celtic Myth and Culture, Lynne Sinclair-Wood
Crystal Clear - A Guide to Quartz Crystal, Jennifer Dent
Crystal Doorways, Simon & Sue Lilly
Dragons of the West, Nigel Pennick
Earth Harmony - Places of Power, Holiness & Healing, Nigel Pennick
Earth Magic, Margaret McArthur
Eildon Tree (The) Romany Language & Lore, Michael Hoadley
Enchanted Forest - The Magical Lore of Trees, Yvonne Aburrow
Eternal Priestess, Sage Weston
Everything You Always Wanted To Know About Your Body, But So Far Nobody's Been Able To Tell You, Chris Thomas & D Baker
Face of the Deep - Healing Body & Soul, Penny Allen

Fairies in the Irish Tradition, Molly Gowen
Familiars - Animal Powers of Britain, Anna Franklin
Forest Paths - Tree Divination, Brian Harrison, Ill. S. Rouse
From Past to Future Life, Dr Roger Webber
Gardening For Wildlife Ron Wilson
God Year, The, Nigel Pennick & Helen Field
Goddess on the Cross, Dr George Young
Goddess Year, The, Nigel Pennick & Helen Field
Goddesses, Guardians & Groves, Jack Gale
Handbook For Pagan Healers, Liz Joan
Handbook of Fairies, Ronan Coghlan
Healing Book, The, Chris Thomas and Diane Baker
Healing Homes, Jennifer Dent
Healing Stones, Sue Philips
Herb Craft - Shamanic & Ritual Use of Herbs, Lavender & Franklin
Hidden Heritage - Exploring Ancient Essex, Terry Johnson
In Search of Herne the Hunter, Eric Fitch
Inner Celtia, Alan Richardson & David Annwn
Intuitive Journey, Ann Walker Isis - African Queen, Akkadia Ford
Kecks, Keddles & Kesh - Celtic Lang & The Cog Almanac, Bayley
Legend of Robin Hood, The, Richard Rutherford-Moore
Lid Off the Cauldron, Patricia Crowther
Light From the Shadows - Modern Traditional Witchcraft, Gwyn
Living Tarot, Ann Walker
Lore of the Sacred Horse, Marion Davies
Lost Lands & Sunken Cities (2nd ed.), Nigel Pennick
Magic of Herbs - A Complete Home Herbal, Rhiannon Ryall
Magical Guardians - Exploring the Spirit and Nature of Trees, Philip Heselton
Magical History of the Horse, Janet Farrar & Virginia Russell
Magical Lore of Animals, Yvonne Aburrow
Magical Lore of Cats, Marion Davies
Magical Lore of Herbs, Marion Davies
Magick Without Peers, Ariadne Rainbird & David Rankine
Masks of Misrule - Horned God & His Cult in Europe, Nigel Jackson
Medicine For The Coming Age, Lisa Sand MD
Menopausal Woman on the Run, Jaki da Costa
Mirrors of Magic - Evoking the Spirit of the Dewponds, P Heselton
Moon Mysteries, Jan Brodie
Mysteries of the Runes, Michael Howard
Mystic Life of Animals, Ann Walker
Pagan Feasts - Seasonal Food for the 8 Festivals, Franklin & Phillips
Patchwork of Magic - Living in a Pagan World, Julia Day
Pathworking - A Practical Book of Guided Meditations, Pete Jennings
Personal Power, Anna Franklin
Pickingill Papers - The Origins of Gardnerian Wicca, Bill Liddell
Pillars of Tubal Cain, Nigel Jackson

Places of Pilgrimage and Healing, Adrian Cooper
Practical Divining, Richard Foord
Practical Meditation, Steve Hounsome
Psychic Self Defence - Real Solutions, Jan Brodie
Real Fairies, David Tame
Reality - How It Works & Why It Mostly Doesn't, Rik Dent
Romany Tapestry, Michael Houghton
Runic Astrology, Nigel Pennick
Sacred Animals, Gordon MacLellan
Sacred Celtic Animals, Marion Davies, Ill. Simon Rouse
Sacred Dorset - On the Path of the Dragon, Peter Knight
Sacred Grove - The Mysteries of the Forest, Yvonne Aburrow
Sacred Geometry, Nigel Pennick
Sacred Ring - Pagan Origins of British Folk Festivals, M. Howard
Season of Sorcery - On Becoming a Wisewoman, Poppy Palin
Seasonal Magic - Diary of a Village Witch, Paddy Slade
Secret Places of the Goddess, Philip Heselton
Secret Signs & Sigils, Nigel Pennick
Spirits of the Earth, Jaq D Hawkins
Stony Gaze, Investigating Celtic Heads John Billingsley
Subterranean Kingdom, The, revised 2nd ed, Nigel Pennick
Symbols of Ancient Gods, Rhiannon Ryall
Talking to the Earth, Gordon MacLellan
The Other Kingdoms Speak, Helena Hawley
Tree: Essence, Spirit & Teacher, Simon & Sue Lilly
Torch and the Spear, Patrick Regan
Warriors at the Edge of Time, Jan Fry
Water Witches, Tony Steele
Way of the Magus, Michael Howard
Weaving a Web of Magic, Rhiannon Ryall
West Country Wicca, Rhiannon Ryall
Wildwitch - The Craft of the Natural Psychic, Poppy Palin
Wildwood King , Philip Kane
Wondrous Land - The Faery Faith of Ireland by Dr Kay Mullin
Working With the Merlin, Geoff Hughes
Your Talking Pet, Ann Walker

FREE detailed catalogue and FREE 'Inspiration' magazine
Contact: Capall Bann Publishing, Auton Farm, Milverton, Somerset, TA4 1NE